MW01052894

IG-88
12-inch vintage Star Wars
$400 loose, $800 in package

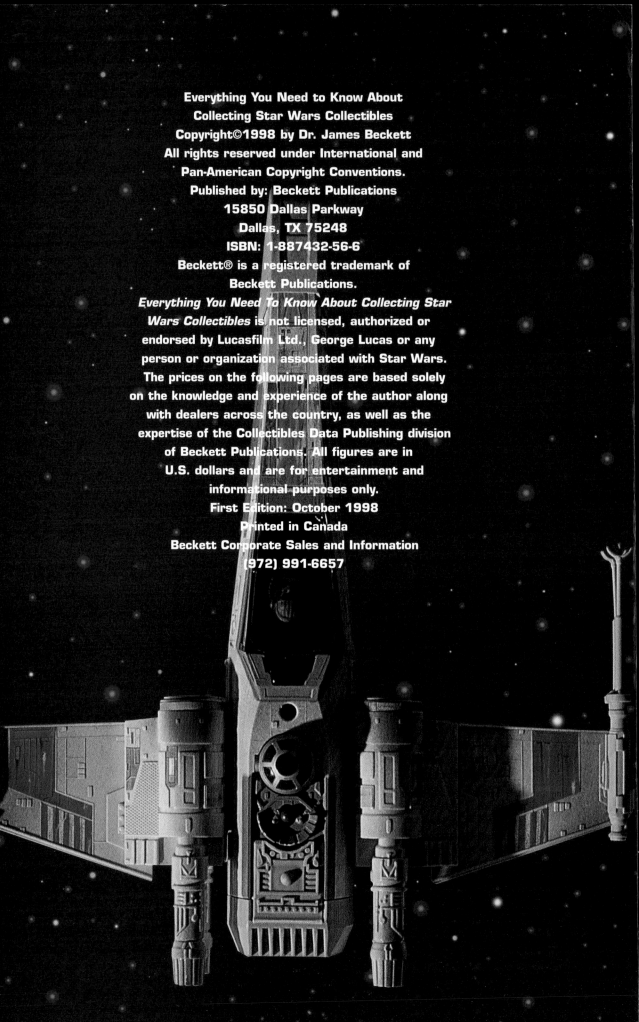

Everything You Need to Know About
Collecting Star Wars Collectibles
Copyright©1998 by Dr. James Beckett
All rights reserved under International and
Pan-American Copyright Conventions.

Published by: Beckett Publications
15850 Dallas Parkway
Dallas, TX 75248
ISBN: 1-887432-56-6
Beckett® is a registered trademark of
Beckett Publications.

Everything You Need To Know About Collecting Star Wars Collectibles is not licensed, authorized or endorsed by Lucasfilm Ltd., George Lucas or any person or organization associated with Star Wars. The prices on the following pages are based solely on the knowledge and experience of the author along with dealers across the country, as well as the expertise of the Collectibles Data Publishing division of Beckett Publications. All figures are in U.S. dollars and are for entertainment and informational purposes only.

First Edition: October 1998
Printed in Canada
Beckett Corporate Sales and Information
(972) 991-6657

STAR WARS
C O L L E C T I B L E S

BY AARON DERR

Like everybody else (in their right mind), Brian Semling, author of *Everything You Need To Know About Collecting Star Wars Collectibles*, grew up loving everything about "Star Wars."

He bought the toys, took them out of the packages and played with them in the yard, in the sandbox, in the street. Some were broken. Some lost. The rest sold at a garage sale. And for a while, "Star Wars" was forgotten. Then, sometime in the early '90s, it all came back.

"I was watching TV one night, and 'Return of the Jedi' just happened to be on," Semling says. "It brought back the nostalgia of being a kid again. I remembered how much I liked the films, and how much I liked the toys."

And just as Brian was getting his Star Wars-collecting feet wet, the market exploded. There was the 1991 release of "Heir to the Empire," the first of three novels by science fiction author Timothy Zahn that served as the licensed continuation of the Star Wars saga. Then there was the 1997 re-release of the original trilogy of films, a Special Edition of "Star Wars" that got everybody fired up again.

And now, as Star Wars memorabilia collecting reaches a fevered pitch, official word has come of a new series of films. "Star Wars: Episode I" hits theaters in the spring of 1999.

"I always liked the idea of the good guy versus the bad guy," Semling says. "There was always a certain element of the Star Wars characters that you could relate to. It's not exactly a realistic film, but it's not totally impossible, either. It's something that could really have happened a long time ago, in a galaxy far, far away."

And at the heart of it all is a bunch of people who just love toys. You have to admit, at the least, those things are pretty cool. The 3 3/4-inch Luke Skywalker with the yellow lightsaber that telescoped out of the hand was no match for what any other kid called an action figure. And whoever owned the 12-inch Boba Fett had one of the more intimidating playthings on the block.

Star Wars collecting is, in a word, huge. There are people who will do anything within reason for a vinyl-caped Jawa. And can you blame them? How could you resist the chance to own a piece of one of the most celebrated, influential, trend-setting, ground-breaking films ever?

"Star Wars" is, in its simplest and purest form, a wonderful, fascinating story. It's a classic mythological tale about good guys and bad guys, and everything the bad guys can do wrong, and everything the good guys can do to stop them.

It's about why it's OK to follow your dreams if you're unhappy with the life you currently lead, and how a lightsaber is better than that clumsy, random blaster any day.

It's about why you must be sure and wait until you're ready to confront your demons, and how a Tauntaun can actually smell worse on the inside.

It's about why, in the end, it's OK to have faith in your friends, and how it's OK to seek out the good in others.

Inside the pages of this book is everything you need to know about collecting Star Wars collectibles. This is how you can join that wonderful universe. So read on. Beware of the Dark Side. Don't be afraid to take your toys out of the boxes and play with them. Take them into the yard, or the sandbox, if you wish.

And, of course, know in your heart that the Force will be with you . . .

Always.

Aaron Derr, an editor with Beckett Publications, still remembers getting out of school early and standing in line for hours the first time he saw "Star Wars." His favorite collectibles, a 3 3/4-inch C-3PO and R2-D2 from the vintage original Star Wars line, sit next to his computer terminal at work.

EVERYTHING
YOU NEED TO KNOW ABOUT
COLLECTING

STAR WARS

C O L L E C T I B L E S

INTRODUCTION	6
HOW TO COLLECT STAR WARS MEMORABILIA	20
VINTAGE ACTION FIGURES	30
LOOSE FIGURES PRICE GUIDE	38
CARDED FIGURES PRICE GUIDE	54
12-INCH FIGURES PRICE GUIDE	102
POWER OF THE FORCE COINS PRICE GUIDE	102
NEW ACTION FIGURES	116
LOOSE FIGURES PRICE GUIDE	122
CARDED FIGURES PRICE GUIDE	142
12-INCH FIGURES PRICE GUIDE	166
VEHICLES, PLAY SETS, ACCESORIES AND DIE-CAST	174
VINTAGE VEHICLES PRICE GUIDE	180
NEW VEHICLES PRICE GUIDE	180
DIE-CAST VEHICLES PRICE GUIDE	186
VINTAGE PLAY SETS PRICE GUIDE	192
NEW PLAY SETS PRICE GUIDE	197
EVERYTHING ELSE	206
CHECKLIST	212

STAR WARS

COLLECTIBLES

The Star Wars universe came to life, in a way no one could ever have possibly imagined, on May 25, 1977. In the days after the George Lucas film was released in two U.S. cities to sell-out crowd after sell-out crowd, the euphoria spread. Within weeks, "Star Wars" was dominating theaters around the country, and in doing so, capturing the hearts of millions of fans.

The film was aimed at male adolescents, but it proved to be popular among all groups. Why?

"Star Wars" is based on a fairly basic mythological model. Most myths have several similar elements, including a good, innocent, and perhaps unlikely hero; a decisively evil and overwhelming force that the hero must overcome; and other usual suspects such as adventure, intrigue and romance. And that's just the highlights.

"Star Wars" takes the basic elements of a successful myth and transplants them into what was at the time a whole new element: outer space. Add to the mix revolutionary special effects, a brilliant supporting cast of creative aliens and exotic venues, a good core of actors, a great cre-

The vintage large replicas of Star Wars vehicles are still sought after by collectors, and for good reason: The AT-AT is worth $125 loose.

ator / director, and enthusiastic and memorable music, and you have one of the greatest and successful epic stories of all time.

"Star Wars" reached to the heart of millions of kids (and adults who wished to be kids again) and enticed their imaginations with a story that invites you in and instantly makes you feel as if it is real. As a child, I remember thinking there could not possibly be any greater toy than that of a working lightsaber. The grace and power of the lightsaber tapped into the desire of every child to fight and conquer evil villains.

The flamboyant Han Solo was probably the most enjoyable character and was realistic enough in his strengths and faults to become the favorite among most males.

Luke Skywalker was the innocent farm boy who always did what his conscience told him, and often tried to sway others to act in the prop-

er light. Ben Kenobi was the mysterious teacher who was respected in spite of his unimpressive appearance. And of course, Darth Vader was the perfect villain, clad in black with the most powerful of voices and the most ominous appearance. With the unparalleled success of the movie came an insatiable demand for Star Wars products of all kinds. Due to the lack of anticipation of such overwhelming consumer lust, very few licensed products were available during 1977.

That soon changed. The major force behind the manufacturing of Star Wars memorabilia was Kenner, a company that produced a few puzzles and board games just in time for Christmas of 1977.

The most popular line of Kenner products was the set of action figures based on an average height of 3 3/4-inches. These figures were not ready in time for Christmas 1977, so Kenner pro-

Die-cast replicas such as this X-Wing aren't as popular as the larger vehicles, but there's no denying Yak Face, which will go for $175 loose and a whopping $2,000 in the box.

Boba Fett is still one of the trilogy's most popular characters. His 12-inch figure lists at $200 loose. A variation of Han Solos (notice the size of the head) makes things interesting for heads-up collectors.

duced a mail-in certificate, known as the Early Bird certificate, which could be redeemed for four action figures as soon as they became available in early 1978.

This first Kenner toy product included four action figures packaged in small plastic bags and then placed in a white tray and mailer box. The four figures included Luke with a telescoping lightsaber, Princess Leia, R2-D2, and Chewbacca with a green crossbow.

Shortly after the Early Bird Kits were produced, Kenner released a set of 12 action figures on cardboard cards with plastic bubbles. The first set included Luke Skywalker, Han Solo, Princess Leia, Obi-Wan Kenobi, Darth Vader, C-3PO, R2-D2, Jawa, Stormtrooper, Death Squad Commander, Tusken Raider and Chewbacca.

To this day, the most valuable of the first 12 are the vinyl-caped Jawa and the Han Solo. The first Jawa was produced with a vinyl or plastic cape

similar to Ben Kenobi's but was soon changed to a more aesthetically pleasing cloth cape. Due to very low production numbers, the vinyl-caped Jawa has become one of the most sought after Star Wars collectibles today. In the package it will command between $2,000 and $4,000.

The Han Solo figure was originally produced with a smaller head that was changed to a regular-sized head toward the end of the of the 12-back release. The small-head Han Solo is typically more popular and will sell for $400-$700, but the large-head Han Solo is rarer and usually will sell for slightly higher.

After the release, and ensuing success, of the first 12 figures, Kenner released eight new figures. Eventually Boba Fett was to become the 21st figure and was released on a Star Wars card even though he was never seen in the first Star Wars movie. Boba Fett has proven to be one of the most popular Star Wars characters over the years. Though his on-camera time is minimal, he has a great appeal due to his image, skill and reputation. The Star Wars Boba Fett, his first issued figure, will sell for about $1,200.

Toys other than the 3 3/4-inch action figures were produced by Kenner in the late 1970s, including several action play sets and various vehicles and accessories designed to accompany the action figures. The play sets helped to fully recreate scenes from the movie with the Death Star, the Cantina and the desert of Tatooine. Most of the influential and memorable space vehicles from the movie were recreated, such as the Millennium Falcon, the Landspeeder, the Tie Fighter, Darth Vader's Tie Fighter, the X-Wing and the Sandcrawler.

Besides toys for the 3 3/4-inch line, Kenner also produced a 12-inch action figure line. The well-done series of 12-inch figures were too large to make vehicles or play sets for, and over

This AT-ST, along with the other large accessories, was designed to hold 3 3/4-inch action figures. The new Luke vs. Wampa set is already proving to be a hot item.

The new large vehicles feature more detailed battle scars than the older versions of the same toy. This X-Wing, with its familiar-looking R2-unit on board, lists at $10 loose, $30 in the package.

time did not prove to be as popular as the 3 3/4-inch figures. The line was discontinued after the release of IG-88 in 1980.

But shortly thereafter, the 12-inch figures became collectibles. By 1985, figures such as the IG-88, Boba Fett and Han Solo were already selling for hundreds of dollars in mint-sealed boxes. Today, the 12-inch line is very popular due to its high quality and level of nostalgia. The rarest of the 12-inch figures (and perhaps, along with Boba Fett, the coolest) is the IG-88, which is valued at $8000-$1,000 in a mint-sealed box.

Even out of the package, IG-88 will sell for around $400.

In 1980, Lucas released "The Empire Strikes Back," which at the time was the most successful sequel in movie history. Though it grossed less than "Star Wars" and "Return of the Jedi," a large contingent of fans consider the second Star Wars film to be their favorite.

The second part of a trilogy is always difficult and usually ends without a decisive conclusion. "The Empire Strikes Back" was no different, as the Rebel heroes start the film in a struggle for

existence and end it barely surviving to fight another day. The film is filled with many great twists, such as Darth Vader's revelation that he is Luke's father, and introduces many new memorable characters, such as the instantly recognizable Yoda.

"The Empire Strikes Back" spawned a whole new wave of memorabilia, featuring 29 new action figures along with many play sets, vehicles and accessories. Also for "The Empire Strikes Back," a new collection was produced called the Micro Collection, which consisted of small plastic play sets and vehicles with 1-inch die-cast metal figures. The idea was moderately successful but was discontinued in 1982 before the release of the next Star Wars film.

The exciting conclusion to the trilogy, "Return of the Jedi," was highly anticipated and delivered strongly. Originally, it was to be called Revenge of the Jedi, and a limited amount of items produced with a Revenge of the Jedi logo have become highly collectible today. The film was the perfect conclusion to the greatest trilogy of all time: the classic struggle of good finally

overcoming evil in a fight to the death. The special effects were even better. And, of course, the Ewoks were a new alien race to be loved by all kids and collectors.

After "Return of the Jedi" and the ensuing release of related memorabilia, another series of Kenner action figures was launched. Called Power of the Force, each figure in the series came with an aluminum collector's coin. Overall, the packing was very well done, which has helped to make it very popular today.

Some of the rarest of all of the Star Wars figures are included in the Power of the Force line. Not as many figures were produced compared to those from the other series due to lack of demand in 1984 and shortly thereafter, but this relatively low level of production has made the line quite

valuable in and out of the package. In the package, Anakin Skywalker and Yak Face will sell for $1,500 to $2,500 each. Out of the package, Yak Face will sell for more than $150 and the Luke Skywalker in Stormtrooper Disguise will sell for about $100 to $150.

Also in 1984, Kenner released a series of Ewoks cartoon series figures and Droids cartoon series figures related to the children's cartoon TV series. Though the shows were never very popular, the figures have proven to be quite in demand. By far the most sought after piece from these two lines is the Boba Fett on Droids card, which will sell for more than $600.

After 1984, there was a lull in Star Wars collecting that lasted nearly 10 years. Star Wars toys and memorabilia simply sat on the shelves dur-

The AT-AT Driver, along with the other new large figures and ships, shows impressive detail, making them early favorites among collectors.

COLLECTOR SERIES

D ue to special conditions such as gravity fluctuation or unusual planetary magnetic fields, the Empire needed a vehicle which could be used on all terrains. Designers resorted to ancient technology and applied it to a large scale for combat vehicles. The finished AT-AT (All Terrain Armored Transport) walkers surpassed Imperial expectations, virtually unstoppable as weapons platforms.

Acting as transports for Imperial ground troops and light vehicles, these beastly machines were used to crush and demoralize enemy forces, thereby forming the core of many Imperial ground assaults.

Driving an Imperial All Terrain Armored Transport requires great skill which can only be acquired through rigorous training and practice. "Ground pilots" train in teams of two, learning to operate the behemoths in conjunction with a combat coordinator. While one pilot drives the monstrous machine, the second pilot assists as a navigator and gunner.

General Veers, when assembling his legion of "Hunters," chose only the best-trained and best-equipped troops in the Imperial Army. During their training, the teams live and work in their walker over much of each mission. The trainees even get involved with the maintenance of the AT-AT walker.

The command crew works in the compact, crowded cockpit which is located in the "head" of the machine. The weapons are also located in this section, as well as holographic targeting systems which allow the gunner and driver a 360° view of their position. The crew is trained to use the walkers for blatant "shock" attacks, landing at great distances but in plain sight of the enemy.

It was this machine monster and its group of flawlessly trained crews that carried out the devastating assault on Hoth.

Authentically styled straight from *The Empire Strikes Back*, the AT-AT driver features his highly detailed, adverse weather protection suit complete with helmet, chest respirator, boots, comlink and Imperial blaster. This special edition 12" figure, available for the first time ever, is destined to become a classic collectible.

MAY THE FORCE BE WITH YOU!

STAR WARS
COLLECTOR SERIES

STAR WARS

STAR WARS
COLLECTOR SERIES

AT-AT DRIVER

AT-AT DRIVER
GALACTIC EMPIRE

GALACTIC EMPIRE

• FULLY POSEABLE FIGURE!

• AUTHENTICALLY STYLED
OUTFIT & ACCESSORIES!

Collectors are
often tempted to
pursue some
obscure variations,
such as the elusive
vinyl-caped Jawa
(replica shown
here). Chewbacca
came with a blue
or green crossbow.

ing the mid-80s, and no new items were produced. Interest began to soar again with the
release of a trilogy of books by Timothy Zahn
starting in 1992. Speculation continued to grow
over the next Star Wars trilogy, and Star Wars
collecting, especially concerning the 3 3/4-inch
action figures and accessories, again grew rapid-
ly.

In 1995, Kenner began to produce a new line of
3 3/4-inch action figures that has continued very
strongly to the present. In 1996, Kenner began a
new 12-inch action figure series that has grown
in popularity since its inception. Many newer
Kenner toys have already been selling for many
times their original retail value. For instance, a
Luke Skywalker: Jedi Knight figure with the
brown vest will sell for $50 to $70 (originally $5)
and a 12-inch Chewy will sell for $50 to $100
(originally $20).

The re-release of the Star Wars trilogy in early
1997 created a new level of excitement in the
area of Star Wars collectibles, and an incredible
surge of new collectors entered the marketplace.
Prices of Star Wars collectibles has steadily
increased, and with the new trilogy on the horizon, a steady increase over the next several years
can be expected.

The first films, actually Episodes IV, V and VI
in a much longer story by Lucas, was for many
of us more than a set of three movies. It was a
fantasy world in which our dreams of adventure
and excitement could be lived out through our
friends Luke, Leia, Han, Chewy and the rest of
the gang. And now we wait for Episode I and the
new Star Wars prequels.

We're certainly ready for the release of another
great trilogy which we hope will also reach a new
level of historic proportion. The new films will not
replace the existing trilogy, but hopefully add to it.
We wait like those kids more than 20 years ago to
see, once again, the famous opening phrase, "A
long time ago, in a galaxy far, far away …"

HOW TO COLLECT
STAR WARS
COLLECTIBLES

How does one go about collecting Star Wars items? What is the best way? What is the right way? Beginning Star Wars collectors should start with items that are most appealing to them. If Darth Vader is your favorite character, then begin with Darth Vader items, from the 3 3/4-inch action figures to the 12-inch figures. It is probably best to start with less expensive items, rather than the rarest and most expensive of figures, as you are getting a feel for collecting.

Does size matter? The 12-inch Darth Vader (right) is harder to find and worth more than the small figure.

After collecting for a few weeks, or months, and talking with fellow Star Wars enthusiasts and dealers, you will begin to see how other people collect so that you can better decide what pattern is best for you. Some people try to collect one of everything that has ever been made. Others focus just on a character such as Darth Vader or Boba Fett.

You may choose to collect solely variations or rare items. Or you may choose to concentrate on a specific part of the universe that is Star Wars toys and try to complete a specific set. A common example would be to collect the first 12 figures either in or out of the package. A loose set of 12 will run just more than $200, while a complete set of carded items will run $2,000 to more than $3,000. My advice is to start with what you like and start small enough that you won't regret your purchase later.

Should one collect in or out of the package? The answer depends on the collector. Do you prefer mint unopened toys or out-of-package items that can be displayed and set up. Also, consider that packaged items will typically cost at least twice as much as unpackaged items. Many collectors ultimately decided to collect items both in and out of the package.

The value is simply a result of supply and demand. An item's value will be determined by the willingness of collectors to buy and sell that item. If many people are interested in buying a specific item and its supply is limited, then the price will tend to increase. If more people are selling a specific item than buying it, the price will go down.

Items such as the vinyl-caped Jawa get almost all of their value from scarcity, or low supply. However, the low availability itself will in turn

The new vehicles, such as Darth Vader's Tie Fighter, might offer more gadgets and gizmos, but there's still something appealing about the older items, such as the original Ben Kenobi.

often raise the demand for the item. For example, many people want to own the vinyl-caped Jawa or Power of the Force Anakin Skywalker because they are so rare. Some items are not incredibly rare, like most of the Boba Fett memorabilia, but due to the incredible demand, are valued much higher than similar items for other characters.

The price guide in *Everything You Need To Know About Collecting Star Wars Collectibles* is based on current market values for complete items out of the package and mint items in the original package. Of course, prices will vary greatly by condition.

Most action figure toys will be graded on a "C" scale of 1-10. Perfect mint is a 10, whereas 9 is a near-mint to mint condition. The listed prices in this book are for items in C9 condition. The item does not need to be perfect to be a 9, but it must be clean and free of obvious and noticeable flaws. A C8 piece will have some noticeable wear, but overall will be in a very presentable condition. A C7 collectible will typically denote something

R2-D2 got its sensorscope after "The Empire Strikes Back," but Han Solo made sure Greedo wouldn't need any updates after "Star Wars."

that is an average condition and will have noticeable wear, but will not be broken or have any detrimental flaws. With a C6 item, you'll see even more prevalent wear, but the piece is still intact. An item in the C5 range is fairly damaged, and by the time we get to C1, the piece is no longer considered to be in collectible condition.

Finally, though most collecting is done for fun, one should keep in mind that buying Star Wars toys and memorabilia is also an investment. It is very possible that the prices will fluctuate, though most items have tended to increase in value over time. Certainly, there is no guarantee of what will happen to prices over time, and collectibles are not recommended to be seen strictly as investments.

However, it can be very fun to watch the value of your collection appreciate over the years.

Figure variations always keep things interesting. The first Snaggletooth was incorrectly tall and blue before the more accurate short red figure came out. This Bespin Security Guard also came as a black figure.

The Millennium Falcon remains one of the trilogy's most popular ships. The new Falcon toy features extra lights, sounds and battle scars that weren't available with the vintage piece.

Power Droid
3 3/4-inch Star Wars
$10 loose, $125 in package

VINTAGE
ACTION FIGURES &
PRICE GUIDE

From the vinyl-caped Jawa
to the Luke Skywalker with the telescoping
lightsaber, nothing compares
to the original Star Wars action figures.

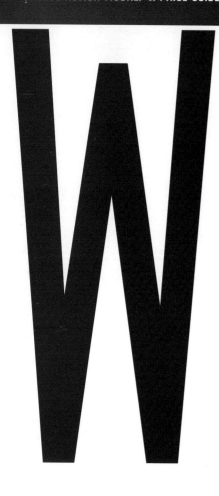hen collecting the older 3 3/4-inch Star Wars action figures, the ones released from 1977 to 1985, the first thing to look at is the condition of the piece. Obviously, for items this old, it's getting harder and harder to find collections fully intact, in good condition and with all the appropriate weapons.

For most people, the items need to be in close-to-mint condition. One thing that's important to realize is that once the figures are out of the package, you can't always tell which package they came from. For instance, a Darth Vader from the Star Wars series in a Star Wars package is exactly the same as a Darth Vader from a The Empire Strikes Back package or a Return of the Jedi package.

In the Star Wars series, three pieces are the most expensive and the most sought after by collectors: the vinyl-caped Jawa, the Luke Skywalker with the telescoping lightsaber and the blue Snaggletooth that came in the Sears Cantina Adventure Set.

With the Jawa, only a limited number were produced with the vinyl cape before the manufacturers went with a cloth-like cape. With scarcity came plenty of demand, and the value of the vinyl-caped Jawa skyrocketed. The scenario for the Luke with the telescoping lightsaber is similar: after a few shipments, the lightsaber was glued in and could not be retracted.

The blue Snaggletooth is rare because it was only available in the Sears set. It was never released on a card, so it's only available loose out of the package, although some collectors try to find it in its original Kenner plastic bag. Later Snaggletooth figures, released on cards in the regular sets, were red and are still popular but much more available and therefore less valuable.

The Power of the Force series was an extra set of figures that came out well after the release of "Return of the Jedi." They were not related to a particular movie and basically included several of the char-

See-Threepio (C-3PO)
3 3/4-inch Star Wars
$15 loose, $150 in package

Death Squad Commander
3 3/4-inch Star Wars
$12 loose, $225 in package

acters that had been left out of the earlier series. Most collectors agree that they're very nice looking pieces, and the coins that they came with make them unique.

This series was produced in 1984, just when Star Wars collecting was starting to fade in popularity. With the lack of demand at the time, there were not very many Power of the Force figures released, so today, they're very much in

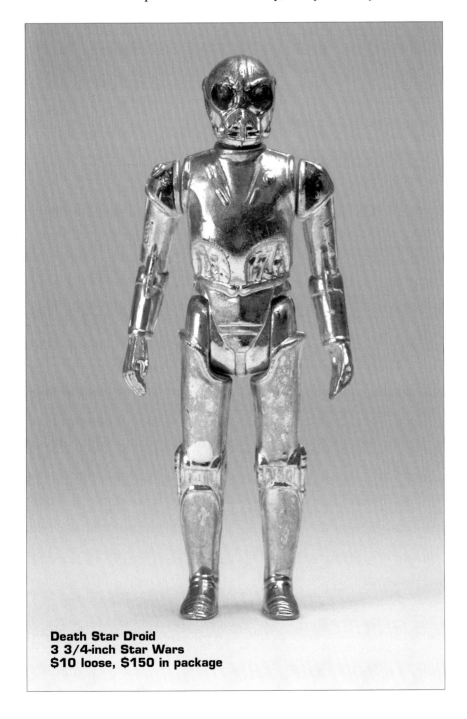

Death Star Droid
3 3/4-inch Star Wars
$10 loose, $150 in package

demand and high in value. A lot of Star Wars collectors at the time didn't bother with the Power of the Force series. The lack of production and high demand translates into higher prices. A lot of the figures from that set are now more valuable than the figures from the original Star Wars set.

The coins that came with the old Power of the Force line are highly collected. Out of 63 coins, only 36 were released with the figures on the cards. The rest had to be purchased via a mail-in to Kenner. At the time, if you called the company, you could have purchased the entire set for $29.99. Now, that same set will sell for $3,000. Each of the mail-in coins go for anywhere from $50 to $100. The Boba Fett coin is worth upwards of $200.

Some of the more popular figures tend to be the ones that didn't have huge roles in the movies, such as Boba Fett. Those rare characters tend to be more mysterious. Although Boba Fett had a somewhat larger role in "Return of the

Jedi" compared to the other bounty hunters introduced in "The Empire Strikes Back," no one could have ever predicted that he would become one of the most popular characters in the entire trilogy.

Boba Fett's popularity comes from his roguish image as the most feared bounty hunter in the galaxy. The occupation of a bounty hunter is certainly intriguing and appealing to young adult males. Boba Fett is in effect an outlaw, and most of all a guy who's really cool.

Another hot commodity is the 12-inch action figures, the most popular of which is the IG-88 figure, along with the Boba Fett and Han Solo pieces. These figures are quite large and, unlike the smaller 3 3/4-inch figures, were never intended to be compatible with ships or play sets or the like. Regardless, they've found quite a home in the hearts of collectors and are becoming more and more popular, even rivaling the popularity of the smaller figures in some circles.

Boba Fett
3 3/4-inch Star Wars
$40 loose, $1,200 in package

VINTAGE TOYS (1977-1985)

LOOSE FIGURES

STAR WARS

Ben (Obi-Wan) Kenobi 15

Boba Fett 40

See-Threepio (C-3PO) 15

Chewbacca. 10

Chewbacca (green crossbow). 25

Darth Vader 12

Death Squad Commander. . . . 12

Death Star Droid 10

Greedo. 10

Hammerhead 8

Han Solo (large head). 30

Han Solo (small head) 40

Jawa (cloth cape). 15

Jawa (vinyl cape) 300

Princess Leia Organa 40

Luke Skywalker (brown hair) . 65

Luke Skywalker (yellow hair) . 30

Luke Skywalker (telescoping lightsaber) 250

Luke Skywalker: X-Wing Pilot. 12

Power Droid. 10

Artoo-Deetoo (R2-D2) 15

R5-D4 10

Sand People. 15

Snaggletooth (blue) 175

Snaggletooth (red). 8

Stormtrooper 15

Walrus Man 10

THE EMPIRE STRIKES BACK

2-1B 12

4-LOM. 15

AT-AT Commander 10

AT-AT Driver. 10

Bespin Security Guard (black). 10

Bespin Security Guard (white) 10

Bossk 8

C-3PO (Removable Limbs) . . . 15

Cloud Car Pilot. 20

Dengar. 10

FX-7. 10

Han Solo (Bespin Outfit). 15

Han Solo (Hoth Battle Gear) . . 15

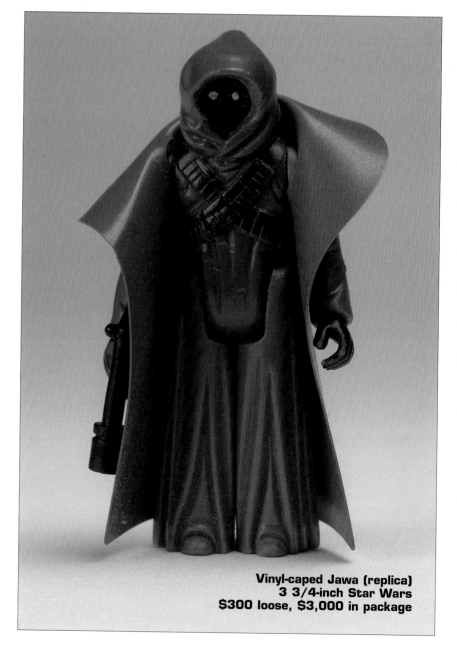

**Vinyl-caped Jawa (replica)
3 3/4-inch Star Wars
$300 loose, $3,000 in package**

Chewbacca
3 3/4-inch Star Wars
$10 loose, $200 in package

Greedo
3 3/4-inch Star Wars
$10 loose, $150 in package

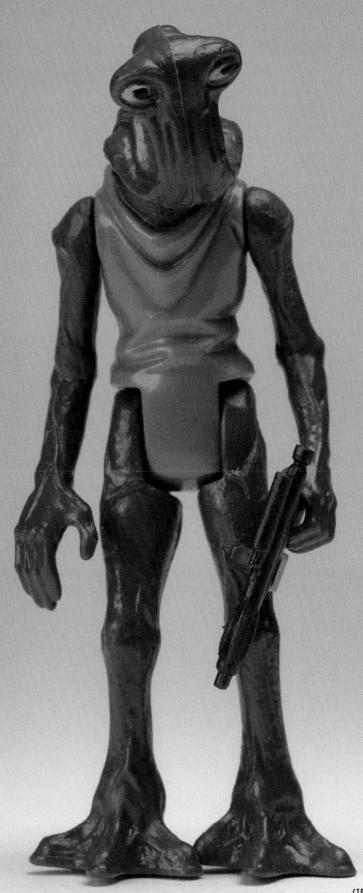

Hammerhead
3 3/4-inch Star Wars
$8 loose, $125 in package

Ben (Obi-Wan) Kenobi
3 3/4-inch Star Wars
$15 loose, $250 in package

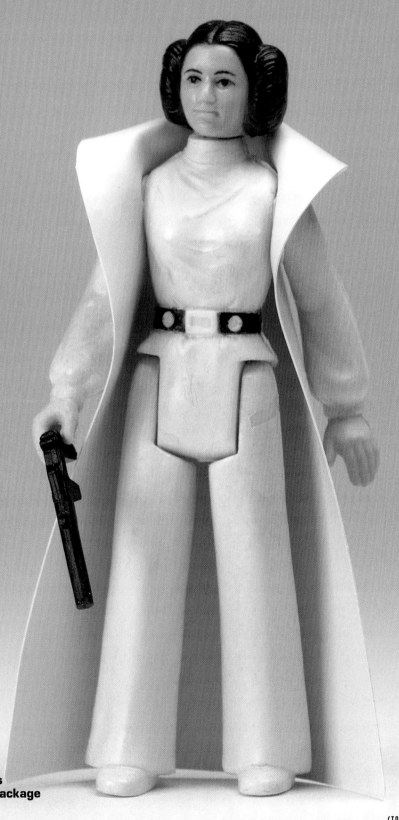

Princess Leia Organa
3 3/4-inch Star Wars
$40 loose, $300 in package

Luke Skywalker
3 3/4-inch Star Wars
$65 loose, $225 in package

Artoo-Deetoo (R2-D2)
3 3/4-inch Star Wars
$15 loose, $150 in package

Imperial Stormtrooper (Hoth Battle Gear) 10

IG-88 15

Imperial Commander 10

Lando Calrissian. 10

Leia Organa (Bespin Gown, crew-neck) 20

Leia Organa (Bespin Gown, turtle-neck) 20

Leia Organa (Hoth Outfit) 20

Lobot. 10

Luke Skywalker (Bespin Fatigues) 20

Luke Skywalker (Hoth Battle Gear) 10

Artoo-Detoo (R2-D2, with sensorscope). 15

Rebel Commander 8

Rebel Soldier (Hoth Battle Gear) 8

Imperial Tie Fighter Pilot. 15

Ugnaught. 8

Yoda (orange snake) 25

Yoda (brown snake) 30

Zuckuss. 8

RETURN OF THE JEDI

8D8 10

Admiral Ackbar 8

AT-ST Driver 8

B-Wing Pilot 8

Bib Fortuna 8

Biker Scout 12

Chief Chirpa 8

The Emperor 8

Emperor's Royal Guard. 10

Gamorrean Guard. 8

General Madine 8

Han Solo (In Trench Coat) . . . 10

Klaatu 10

Klaatu Skiff 10

Lando Calrissian (Skiff Guard

Disguise) 12

Princess Leia Organa (Boushh Disguise) 15

Princess Leia Organa (In Combat Poncho). 30

Lograya 10

Luke Skywalker (Jedi Knight outfit, blue saber) 60

Luke Skywalker (Jedi Knight out-

**Luke Skywalker: X-Wing Pilot
3 3/4-inch Star Wars
$12 loose, $150 in package**

Snaggletooth (blue)
3 3/4-inch Star Wars
$175 loose

Han Solo (large head)
3 3/4-inch Star Wars
$30 loose, $700 in package

R5-D4
3 3/4-inch Star Wars
$10 loose, $100 in package

**Walrus Man
3 3/4-inch Star Wars
$10 loose, $125 in package**

Stormtrooper
3 3/4-inch Star Wars
$15 loose, $250 in package

Sand People
3 3/4-inch Star Wars
$15 loose, $100 in package

Darth Vader
3 3/4-inch Star Wars
$12 loose, $250 in package

fit, green saber) 50

Lumat 20

Nien Numb. 8

Nikto 8

Paploo 20

Prune Face. 8

Rancor Keeper 8

Rebel Commando. 8

Ree-Yees 8

Squid Face 10

Teebo 12

Weequay 25

Wicket W. Warrick 15

POWER OF THE FORCE

Amanaman 125

Anakin Skywalker 30

A-Wing Pilot 40

Barada 50

EV-9D9 75

Han Solo
(In Carbonite Chamber) 100

Imperial Dignitary 25

Imperial Gunner 75

Lando Calrissian
(General Pilot) 10

Luke Skywalker
(In Battle Poncho) 50

Luke Skywalker (Imperial
Stormtrooper Outfit) 150

Artoo-Detoo (R2-D2, with pop-up
Lightsaber) 75

Romba 20

Warok 20

Yak Face 175

CARDED FIGURES

STAR WARS 12-BACKS

Ben Kenobi 250

C-3PO 150

Chewbacca 200

Darth Vader 250

Death Squad Commander . . . 225

Jawa (Vinyl Cape) 3000

Jawa (Cloth cape) 250

Han Solo (large head) 700

**2-1B
3 3/4-inch TESB
$12 loose, $50 in package**

AT-AT Commander
3 3/4-inch TESB
$10 loose, $40 in package

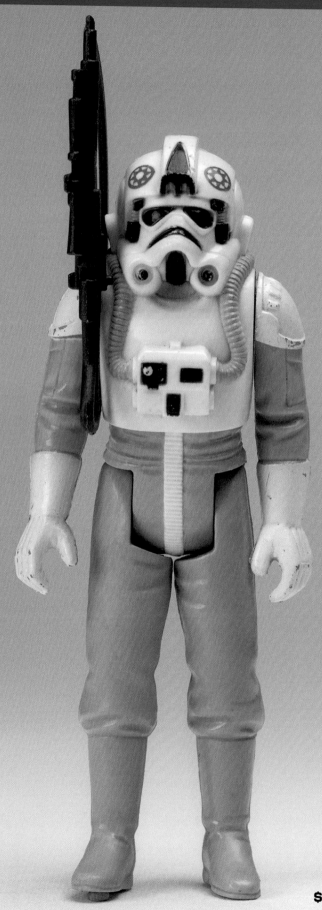

**AT-AT Driver
3 3/4-inch TESB
$10 loose, $60 in package**

Bespin Security Guard
3 3/4–inch TESB
$10 loose, $50 in package

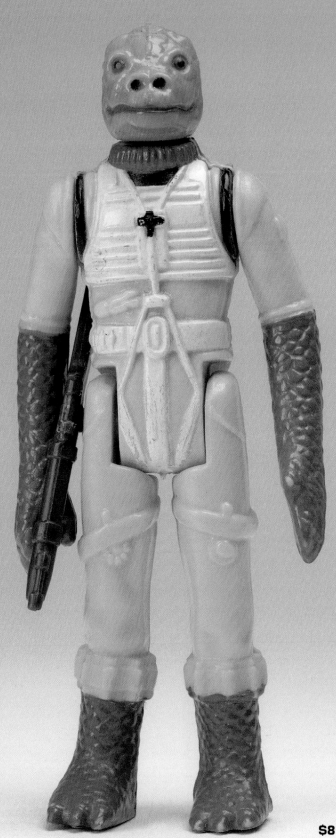

Bossk (Bounty Hunter)
3 3/4-inch Star Wars
$8 loose, $100 in package

No. 50708   Edad: de 4 años en adelante

LA GUERRA DE
EL REGRESO DEL
JEDI
LAS GALAXIAS MR

Lando Calrissian MR

LiLi LEDY

Lando Calrissian (with teeth)
3 3/4-inch TESB
$10 loose, $60 in package

(Twin-Pod) Cloud Car Pilot
3 3/4-inch TESB
$20 loose, $60 in package

Dengar
3 3/4-inch TESB
$10 loose, $50 in package

Han Solo (small head) 500

Princess Leia 300

Luke Skywalker 350

R2-D2 150

Sand Person 250

Stormtrooper 250

STAR WARS 20/21 BACKS

Ben Kenobi. 125

Boba Fett 1200

C-3PO 100

Chewbacca. 125

Darth Vader 125

Death Squad Commander. . . 100

Death Star Droid 150

Jawa (cloth cape) 100

Greedo. 150

Hammerhead 125

Han Solo (large head). 400

Leia 300

Luke 225

Luke Skywalker: X-Wing Pilot 150

Power Droid. 125

R2-D2 100

R5-D4 100

Sand Person 100

Snaggletooth 125

Stormtrooper 150

Walrus Man 125

THE EMPIRE STRIKES BACK

2-1B 50

4-LOM 150

AT-AT Commander 40

AT-AT Driver. 60

Ben Kenobi. 125

Bespin Guard (black) 40

Bespin Guard (white) 50

Boba Fett 300

Bossk. 100

C-3PO 125

C-3PO (Removable Limbs) . . . 60

Chewbacca. 100

Cloud Car Pilot. 60

Darth Vader 80

Death Star Droid 125

Dengar. 50

FX-7. 50

Greedo. 125

FX-7 (Medical Droid)
3 3/4-inch TESB
$10 loose, $50 in package

No. 39020
ASST. #69360

877 60139
TARGET
052 $ 2.49

STAR
THE
EMPIRE
STRIKES BACK
WARS

Greedo®

Kenner®

Meets or exceeds all safety
requirements of Product Standard 72-76

Greedo
3 3/4-inch TESB
$10 loose, $125 in package

**Imperial Commander
3 3/4-inch TESB
$10 loose, $50 in package**

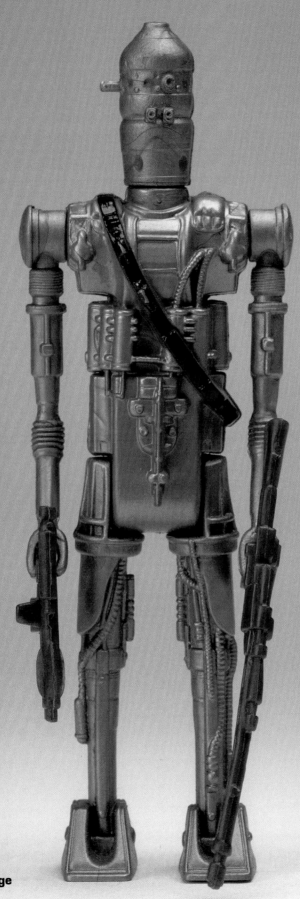

IG-88 (Bounty Hunter)
3 3/4-inch TESB
$15 loose, $100 in package

Stormtrooper (Hoth Gear)
3 3/4-inch Star Wars
$10 loose, $60 in package

Ben (Obi-Wan) Kenobi
3 3/4-inch TESB
$15 loose, $125 in package

Leia Organa (Hoth Outfit)
3 3/4-inch TESB
$20 loose, $200 in package

Rebel Commander
3 3/4-inch TESB
$8 loose, $40 in package

Hammerhead 125

Han Solo 300

Han Solo (Bespin Fatigues). . 125

Han Solo (Hoth Battle Gear) . . 60

Imperial Stormtrooper
(Hoth Battle Gear) 60

IG-88 100

Imperial Commander 50

Jawa 100

Lando Calrissian. 80

Princess Leia Organa 200

Princess Leia Organa
(In Bespin Gown) 200

Princess Leia Organa
(Hoth Battle Gear) 150

Lobot. 40

Luke Skywalker
(brown hair). 200

Luke Skywalker
(yellow hair). 200

Luke Skywalker
(Bespin Outfit) 200

Luke Skywalker
(Hoth Battle Gear) 100

Luke Skywalker:
X-Wing Pilot. 100

Power Droid. 100

Artoo-Detoo (R2-D2) 60

Artoo-Detoo (R2-D2,
with sensorscope) 60

R5-D4 100

Rebel Commander 40

Rebel Soldier 40

Sand Person 100

Star Destroyer Commander . . 75

Stormtrooper 80

Imperial Tie Fighter Pilot. . . . 100

Ugnaught. 50

Walrusman. 125

Yoda (orange snake) 80

Yoda (brown snake) 300

Zuckuss 80

RETURN OF THE JEDI

2-1B 50

4-LOM 40

8D8 40

Admiral Ackbar 40

AT-AT Commander 40

AT-AT Driver. 50

AT-ST Driver. 40

**Rebel Soldier (Hoth Gear)
3 3/4-inch TESB
$8 loose, $40 in package**

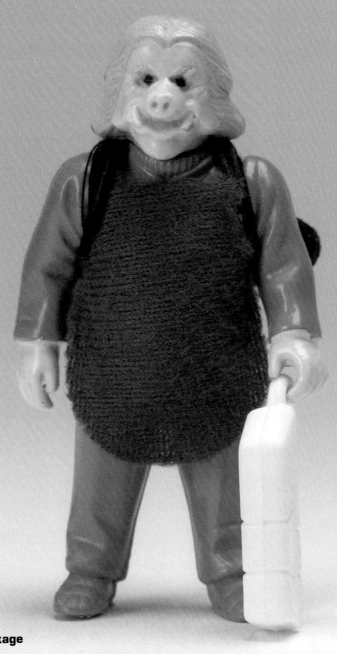

Ugnaught
3 3/4-inch TESB
$8 loose, $50 in package

Luke Skywalker (Bespin Fatigues)
3 3/4-inch TESB
$20 loose, $200 in package

Luke Skywalker (Hoth Gear)
3 3/4-inch TESB
$10 loose, $100 in package

Han Solo (Bespin Outfit)
3 3/4-inch TESB
$15 loose, $125 in package

Han Solo (Hoth Outfit)
3 3/4-inch TESB
$15 loose, $60 in package

Yoda (brown snake)
3 3/4-inch TESB
$30 loose, $300 in package

Lando Calrissian
3 3/4-inch TESB
$10 loose, $80 in package

Ben (Obi-Wan) Kenobi 50

Bespin Guard (black) 50

Bespin Guard (white) 30

Bib Fortuna 40

Biker Scout 50

Boba Fett (desert scene) 275

Boba Fett (space scene) 300

Bossk 80

B-Wing Pilot. 40

C-3PO (Removable Limbs) . . . 40

Chewbacca. 60

Chief Chirpa 40

Cloud Car Pilot. 50

Darth Vader 60

Death Squad Commander. . . . 60

Death Star Droid 80

Dengar. 40

Emperor. 40

Emperor's Royal Guard. 50

FX-7. 50

Gamorrean Guard. 40

General Madine 40

Greedo. 50

Hammerhead 80

Han Solo (Bespin Outfit). . . . 100

Han Solo (Hoth Outfit) 100

Han Solo (large head). 200

Han Solo (In Trench Coat) . . . 50

Imperial Stormtrooper
(Hoth Battle Gear) 50

IG-88. 80

Imperial Commander 40

Klaatu 40

Klaatu (skiff) 40

Lando Calrissian. 50

Lando (In Skiff Disguise) 50

Princess Leia Organa 500

Princess Leia Organa (In Bespin
Gown, turtleneck). 175

Princess Leia Organa
(In Boushh Disguise) 60

Princess Leia Organa
(Combat Poncho). 75

Princess Leia Organa
(Hoth Battle Gear) 125

Lobot. 40

Logray 40

Luke Skywalker
(yellow hair). 200

Luke Skywalker
(Bespin Outfit) 175

4-LOM
3 3/4-inch TESB
$15 loose, $150 in package

8D8
3 3/4-inch Return of the Jedi
$10 loose, $40 in package

Admiral Ackbar
3 3/4-inch Return of the Jedi
$8 loose, $40 in package

AT-ST Driver
3 3/4-inch Return of the Jedi
$8 loose, $40 in package

Biker Scout
3 3/4-inch Return of the Jedi
$12 loose, $50 in package

Gamorrean Guard
3 3/4-inch Return of the Jedi
$8 loose, $40 in package

Chief Chirpa
3 3/4-inch Return of the Jedi
$8 loose, $40 in package

Lando Calrissian (Skiff Disguise)
3 3/4-inch Return of the Jedi
$12 loose, $50 in package

Luke Skywalker

(Hoth Battle Gear) 50

Luke Skywalker (Jedi Knight

outfit, blue saber) 200

Luke Skywalker (Jedi Knight

outfit, green saber) 100

Luke Skywalker:

X-Wing Pilot. 60

Lumat 50

Nien Numb. 40

Nikto 40

Paploo 50

Power Droid. 50

Prune Face. 40

Artoo-Detoo (R2-D2, with

sensorscope) 50

R5-D4 50

Rancor Keeper 40

Rebel Commander 40

Rebel Commando. 40

Rebel Soldier 40

Ree-Yees 40

Sand Person 80

Snaggletooth (red) 50

Squid Head 40

Stormtrooper 60

Teebo. 60

Imperial Tie Fighter Pilot. 75

Ugnaught. 40

Walrus Man 60

Weequay 40

Wicket 60

Yoda (brown snake) 100

Zuckuss 40

POWER OF THE FORCE

Amanaman 250

Anakin Skywalker 2500

AT-AT Driver 700

AT-ST Driver 60

A-Wing Pilot 125

Barada 125

Ben (Obi-Wan) Kenobi 125

B-Wing Pilot 40

The Emperor
3 3/4-inch Return of the Jedi
$8 loose, $40 in package

Bib Fortuna
3 3/4-inch Return of the Jedi
$8 loose, $40 in package

Logray (Ewok Medicine Man)
3 3/4-inch Return of the Jedi
$10 loose, $40 in package

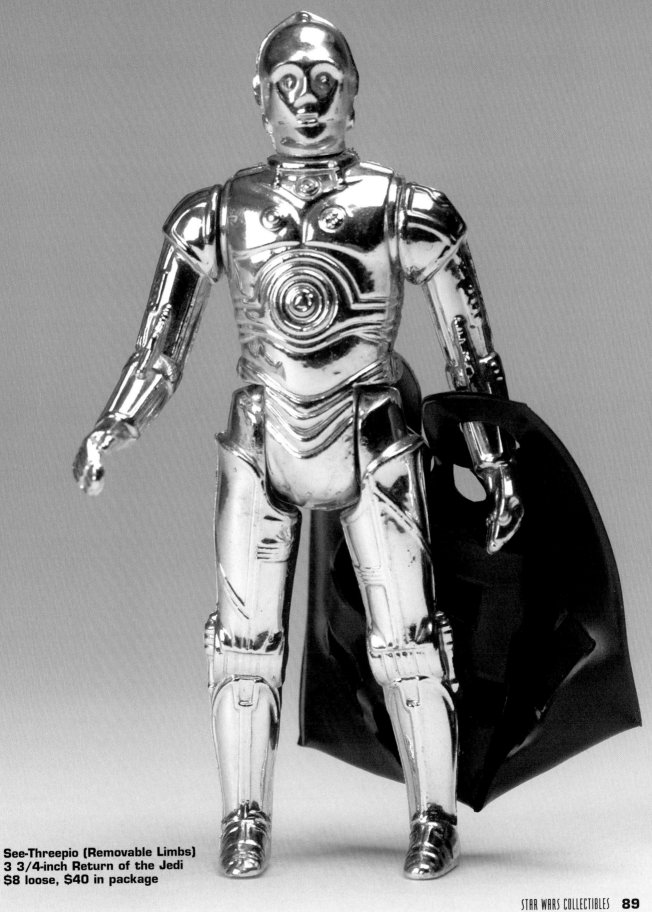

See-Threepio (Removable Limbs)
3 3/4-inch Return of the Jedi
$8 loose, $40 in package

Imperial Tie Fighter Pilot
3 3/4-inch Return of the Jedi
$15 loose, $75 in package

Lobot
3 3/4-inch Return of the Jedi
$10 loose, $40 in package

General Madine
3 3/4-inch Return of the Jedi
$8 loose, $40 in package

Nikto
3 3/4-inch Return of the Jedi
$8 loose, $40 in package

C-3PO (removable limbs) 80

Chewbacca. 100

Darth Vader 100

The Emperor 75

EV-9D9 150

Gamorrean Guard. 250

Han Solo (In Carbonite

Chamber). 250

Han Solo (In Trench Coat) . . 400

Imperial Dignitary 100

Imperial Gunner 150

Jawa 100

Lando Calrissian

(General Pilot) 125

Princess Leia Organa

(In Combat Poncho). 100

Luke Skywalker

(In Battle Poncho) 125

Luke Skywalker

(Jedi Knight Outfit). 275

Luke Skywalker (Imperial

Stormtrooper Outfit). 400

Luke Skywalker:

X-Wing Pilot. 100

Lumat 60

Nikto 600

Paploo. 50

Artoo-Detoo (R2-D2,

with pop-up Lightsaber) 150

Romba. 60

Stormtrooper 225

Teebo. 125

Warok 75

Wicket 200

Yak Face. 2000

Yoda 500

DROIDS CARTOON

STAR WARS

	LOOSE	MIB
A-Wing Pilot	80	250
Boba Fett	250	600
C-3PO	50	125
Jann Tosh	10	25
Jord Dusat	10	25
Kea Moll	10	25
Kez-Iban	10	25
R2-D2	40	100
Sise Fromm	40	100
Thall Joben	10	25
Tig Fromm	30	80

**R2-D2 With Sensorscope
3 3/4-inch Return of the Jedi
$15 loose, $50 in package**

AGES 4 & UP
Asst. No. 69570
No. 69574

STAR WARS

THE POWER OF THE FORCE

R2-D2™
With
Light-Pipe Eye Port and Retractable Leg!

R2-D2
Autographed by
actor Kenny Baker

Nien Numb
3 3/4-inch Return of the Jedi
$8 loose, $40 in package

Rancor Keeper
3 3/4-inch Return of the Jedi
$8 loose, $40 in package

Rebel Commando
3 3/4-inch Return of the Jedi
$8 loose, $40 in package

Ree-Yees
3 3/4-inch Return of the Jedi
$8 loose, $40 in package

No. 70650

Ages 4 and up

STAR WARS
RETURN OF THE
JEDI

Luke Skywalker®
(Jedi Knight® Outfit)

Kenner®
Meets or exceeds all safety
requirements of Product Standard 72-76

0175-203-05

Luke Skywalker (Jedi Knight Outfit)
3 3/4-inch Return of the Jedi
$60 loose, $200 in package

Weequay
3 3/4-inch Return of the Jedi
$25 loose, $40 in package

Uncle Gundy 8 20

12-INCH ACTION FIGURES

	LOOSE	MIB
Han Solo	250	500
Luke Skywalker	150	300
Princess Leia	125	250
Ben Kenobi	200	400
C-3PO	50	125
R2-D2	75	150
IG-88	400	800
Boba Fett	200	400
Jawa	100	200
Stormtrooper	150	300
Darth Vader	80	150
Chewbacca	80	150

COINS

POWER OF THE FORCE

62-coin set	3000
2-1B	150
Amanaman	10
Anakin Skywalker	125
AT-AT	100
AT-ST Driver	20
A-Wing Pilot	8
Barada	8

Bib Fortuna 125
Biker Scout 20
Boba Fett 200
B-Wing Pilot 15
C-3PO 20
Chewbacca 30
Chief Chirpa 40
Creatures 90
Darth Vader 25

Droids 90
Emperor 20
Emperor's Royal Guard 75
EV-9D9 8
FX-7 125
Gamorrean Guard 30
Greedo 125
Han Solo in Hoth Battle Gear . 90
Han Solo 150

**A-Wing Pilot
3 3/4-inch Power of the Force
$40 loose, $125 in package**

B-Wing Pilot
3 3/4-inch Power of the Force
$12 loose, $40 in package

Barada
3 3/4-inch Power of the Force
$50 loose, $125 in package

Lando Calrissian (General Pilot)
3 3/4-inch Power of the Force
$10 loose, $125 in package

**Emperor's Royal Guard
3 3/4-inch Return of the Jedi
$10 loose, $50 in package**

Klaatu
3 3/4-inch Return of the Jedi
$10 loose, $40 in package

Princess Leia (In Combat Poncho)
3 3/4-inch Return of the Jedi
$30 loose, $75 in package

Paploo
3 3/4-inch Return of the Jedi
$20 loose, $50 in package

Han Frozen in Carbonite 10

Han Solo in Trenchcoat. 30

Hoth Solo in Stormtrooper
Disguise. 150

Imperial Commander 75

Imperial Dignitary. 8

Imperial Gunner. 8

Jawas 20

Lando Calrissian in
General Pilot Gear (with
Millenium Falcon in
background) 8

Lando Calrissian
with Cloud City. 75

Princess Leia in
Boushh Disguise 125

Princess Leia in
Combat Poncho 20

Princess Leia with R2-D2 . . . 125

Logray. 40

Luke Skywalker in
Battle Poncho. 8

Luke Skywalker in
Dagobah Fatigues. 150

Luke Skywalker in Hoth Gear 125

Luke Skywalker: Jedi Knight . . 30

Luke Skywalker with Landspeeder
75 . . . .

Luke Skywalker in Stormtrooper
Disguise. 10

Luke Skywalker: X-Wing Pilot . 30

Lumat 5

Millennium Falcon 125

Obi-Wan Kenobi. 30

Paploo. 5

Romba. 5

R2-D2 8

Sail Skiff 200

Star Destroyer Commander . 100

Stormtrooper 30

Teebo. 20

Tie Fighter Pilot 75

Tusken Raider 100

Warok 5

Wicket 25

Yak Face. 125

Yoda 50

Zuckuss 50

**C-3PO
12-inch
$50 loose, $125 in package**

Chewbacca
12-inch
$80 loose, $150 in package

Darth Vader
12-inch
$80 loose, $150 in package

Han Solo
12-inch
$250 loose, $500 in package

Luke Skywalker
12-inch
$150 loose, $300 in package

Princess Leia
12-inch
$125 loose, $250 in package

COLLECTION 2
Asst. No. 69605
No. 69618

STAR WARS®

THE POWER OF THE FORCE

2-1B MEDIC DROID™
with
MEDICAL DIAGNOSTIC COMPUTER

AGES 4 & UP

⚠ **WARNING:**

CHOKING HAZARD–Small parts.
Not for children under 3 years.

Kenner®

2-1B Medic Droid
3 3/4-inch Power of the Force
$2 loose, $6 in package

NEW ACTION FIGURES & PRICE GUIDE

With more detail and more muscle,
the new line of action figures was at first
greeted with some resentment but has since
caught on among Star Wars collectors.

The new Power of the Force series, first released in 1995, was named after the now-popular original Power of the Force series in the mid-'80s. The new set is often referred to as the Power of the Force II series.

Power of the Force II was released about a year and a half before the Special Edition re-release of the trilogy in early 1997. If the mid- to late-'80s was the down cycle of Star Wars collecting, the early '90s was when it picked up steam again. Some credit the renewed interested to the publication of a trilogy of Lusasfilm-licensed books by Timothy Zahn. With the release of the novels came discussion among fans of the original films and the possibility of brand new Star Wars films on the horizon.

With increased discussion of the films came renewed interested in the memorabilia, and Star Wars collecting took off. Interest in collecting Star Wars-related items is at an all-time high, and with the upcoming release of the prequels, there seems to be no limit, especially when one considers the possibility of brand new collectibles with characters related to the new films.

The first thing you notice about the new line of figures is that they're much more muscular and modern-looking. The view of the new figures compared to the old figures has changed in recent years. At first, perhaps there was a little resentment and some people were disappointed. But as the figures have gotten better, collectors are starting to find more room on their shelves for the new toys.

A good example is the new Princess Leia figures. Most people would agree that the first Princess Leia figure released in the '90s was not a good portrayal of Princess Leia, but the following figures truly do bear a strong resemblance, as they should.

Also, the new 12-inch figures have become extremely popular, again rivaling the popularity of the smaller figures. In the new Power of the Force 12-inch collection, the Boba Fett

COLLECTION 2
Asst. No. 69605
No. 69688

STAR WARS

®

THE POWER OF THE FORCE

4-LOM™
with
BLASTER PISTOL AND BLASTER RIFLE

AGES 4 & UP

⚠ **WARNING:**

CHOKING HAZARD–Small parts.
Not for children under 3 years.

4-LOM
3 3/4-inch Power of the Force
$2 loose, $6 in package

COLLECTION 2
Asst. No. 69605
No. 69686

STAR WARS®

THE POWER OF THE FORCE

ADMIRAL ACKBAR™
with
COMLINK WRIST BLASTER

AGES 4 & UP

⚠ **WARNING:**

CHOKING HAZARD–Small parts.
Not for children under 3 years.

Admiral Ackbar
3 3/4-inch Power of the Force
$2 loose, $6 in package

and Chewbacca figures are the most popular and most sought after. Some of the other items might go for a higher price since they were offered exclusively through certain stores and therefore have smaller production figures.

Now, the new figures are widely accepted among Star Wars collectors and are very highly sought after. The quality is certainly excellent. Most collectors can still appreciate the older items while also enjoying the new ones that are different but still a lot of fun.

It's a big change, and perhaps at first the figures were just too much different from the old ones.

Some people probably didn't think it was a good idea to produce new figures in the first place, but in general those feelings have faded and collectors have embraced the new line of products.

AT-ST Driver
3 3/4-inch Power of the Force
$2 loose, $6 in package

NEW TOYS (1995-PRESENT)

LOOSE FIGURES

STAR WARS: POWER OF THE FORCE (1995)

Ben Kenobi (half shot, long lightsaber). 20

Ben Kenobi (full shot, long lightsaber). 20

Ben Kenobi (full shot, short lightsaber). 4

Chewbacca 4

C-3PO. 4

Darth Vader (long lightsaber). . 12

Darth Vader (short lightsaber) . . 4

Darth Vader (short lightsaber, long pack). 8

Han Solo. 4

Luke Skywalker (long lightsaber) 15

Luke Skywalker (short lightsaber). 6

Princess Leia (two bands) 6

Princess Leia (three bands) 8

R2-D2. 4

Stormtrooper. 5

STAR WARS: POWER OF THE

FORCE (1996)

Boba Fett (circle on hand) 4

Boba Fett (half-circle on hand) . 15

Chewbacca 4

Dash Rendar 2

Death Star Gunner (green). 4

Death Star Gunner (red). 8

Greedo (green) 2

Greedo (red) 8

Hammerhead (green). 2

Hammerhead (red) 8

Han Solo (in carbonite) 2

Han Solo (in carbonite and freeze chamber) 5

Han Solo (Hoth open hand) . . . 8

Han Solo (Hoth closed hand) . . 4

Jawa (red). 8

Jawa (green) 3

Ben (Obi-Wan) Kenobi
3 3/4-inch Power of the Force
$20 loose, $50 in package

SPECIAL LIMITED EDITION!

Asst. No.
69675
No. 84022

STAR WARS
THE POWER OF THE FORCE

BESPIN HAN SOLO™

AGES 4 AND UP

⚠ **WARNING:**
CHOKING HAZARD-Small parts.
Not for children under 3 years.

Bespin Han Solo
3 3/4-inch Millenium Mint
$4 loose, $25 in package

THE **Kenner** COLLECTION ™

STAR WARS®

THE POWER OF THE FORCE

FREEZE FRAME™ ACTION SLIDE
ACTUAL MOVIE SCENES TO SEE & PROJECT

STAR WARS®

ROJ

HAN SOLO™
Surrounded by a fierce hunting party of Ewoks.

Works with standard slide projector

⚠ **WARNING:**
CHOKING HAZARD-Small parts.
Not for children under 3 years.

AGES 4 & UP

HAN SOLO™
in ENDOR GEAR
with BLASTER PISTOL

Han Solo in Endor Gear
3 3/4-inch POF with slide
$12 in package

THE **Kenner** COLLECTION™

STAR WARS®

THE POWER OF THE FORCE

FREEZE FRAME™ ACTION SLIDE
ACTUAL MOVIE SCENES TO SEE & PROJECT

STAR WARS®

ESB

LUKE SKYWALKER™
Luke Skywalker ventures into Vader's web on Bespin's Cloud City.

Works with standard slide projector

⚠ **WARNING:**
CHOKING HAZARD-Small parts.
Not for children under 3 years.

AGES 4 & UP

Asst.

COLLECTION 1

WITH DETACHABLE HAND

BESPIN LUKE SKYWALKER™
WITH LIGHTSABER and BLASTER PISTOL

Bespin Luke Skywalker
3 3/4-inch POF with slide
$12 in package

Lando Calrissian 2

Luke Skywalker
(long lightsaber) 10

Luke Skywalker
(short lightsaber) 4

Luke Skywalker
(short lightsaber, long pack) . . . 6

Luke Skywalker: Jedi Knight
(brown vest) 25

Luke Skywalker: Jedi Knight
(black vest) 2

Luke Skywalker in Dagobah
Fatigues (short light saber) 2

Luke Skywalker in Dagobah
Fatigues (long light saber) 5

Luke Skywalker:
Stormtrooper (red) 8

Luke Skywalker:
Stormtrooper (green) 4

Luke Skywalker: X-Wing Pilot
(long lightsaber) 10

Luke Skywalker: X-Wing Pilot
(short lightsaber) 4

Luke Skywalker: X-Wing Pilot
(short saber, long pack) 10

Prince Xizor 2

Princess Leia in
Boussh Disguise 2

R5-D4 (red) 8

R5-D4 (green, straight latch) . . . 8

R5-D4 (green, hook latch) 2

Sandtrooper 4

Tatooine Stormtrooper 8

Tie Fighter (without sticker) 2

Tie Fighter (with sticker) 10

Tusken Raider
(closed, green) 12

Tusken Raider (open, green) . . . 2

Tusken Raider (closed, red) 8

Tusken Raider (open, red) 8

Yoda 4

STAR WARS: POWER OF THE FORCE (TWO-PACKS AND THREE-PACKS, 1996-97)

Ben Kenobi / Darth Vader / Luke
Skywalker 15

Boba Fett / IG-88 15

Chewbacca / Han Solo / Lando

COLLECTION 2
Asst. No. 69605
No. 69812

Bib Fortuna
3 3/4-inch Power of the Force
$2 loose, $6 in package

Biggs Darklighter
3 3/4-inch POF with slide
$6 in package

COLLECTION 1
Asst. No. 69570
No. 69582

STAR WARS®

THE POWER OF THE FORCE

BOBA FETT™
With
Sawed-Off Blaster Rifle and Jet Pack!

AGES 4 & UP

⚠ **WARNING:**

CHOKING HAZARD-Small parts.
Not for children under 3 years.

Kenner

Boba Fett
3 3/4-inch Power of the Force
$4 loose, $10 in package

COLLECTION 2
Asst. No. 69605
No. 69617

STAR WARS®

THE POWER OF THE FORCE

BOSSK™
with
BLASTER RIFLE AND PISTOL

AGES 4 & UP

⚠ **WARNING:**

CHOKING HAZARD–Small parts.
Not for children under 3 years.

Kenner®

Bossk
3 3/4-inch Power of the Force
$2 loose, $6 in package

Calrissian 15

C-3PO / R2-D2 / Stormtrooper . 15

Luke / Tusken Raider / Ben . . . 15

Luke Skywalker / Lando Calrissian

/ Tie Fighter 15

Luke Skywalker / AT-ST Driver /

Princess Leia 15

Xizor / Darth Vader 15

STAR WARS: POWER OF THE FORCE DELUXE PACKS (1996-97)

Boba Fett 4

Crowd Control Stormtrooper . . . 4

Crown Control (w/sticker) 20

Han Solo with Smuggler Flight . . 4

Hoth Rebel Soldier 4

Imperial Probe Droid (orange) . 10

Imperial Probe Droid (green) . . . 4

Luke with Desert Skiff 4

Snowtrooper 4

STAR WARS: POWER OF THE FORCE (1997)

2-1B 2

4-LOM 2

Admiral Ackbar 2

ASP-7 2

AT-ST Driver 2

Bib Fortuna 2

Bossk 2

Dengar 2

Emperor Palpatine 2

Emperor's Royal Guard 2

EV-9D9 2

Gamorrean Guard 2

Grand Moff Tarkin 2

Han Solo in Bespin Fatigues 2

Han Solo in Endor Gear (blue) . . 2

Han Solo in Endor Gear (brown) 2

Hoth Rebel Soldier 2

Hoth Rebel Soldier II 2

Hoth Snowtrooper 2

Lando Calrissian 2

Luke Skywalker Ceremonial 2

Luke Skywalker in

Hoth Battle Gear 2

Luke Skywalker in

Hoth Battle Gear II 2

C-3PO 3 3/4-inch Power of the Force $4 loose, $10 in package

THE **Kenner** COLLECTION™

STAR WARS®

THE POWER OF THE FORCE

FREEZE FRAME™ ACTION SLIDE
ACTUAL MOVIE SCENES TO SEE & PROJECT

STAR WARS®

ESB

CAPTAIN PIETT™
Commanding Darth Vader's flagship *Executor.*

Works with standard slide projector

⚠ **WARNING:**
CHOKING HAZARD–Small parts.
Not for children under 3 years.

AGES 4 & UP

CAPTAIN PIETT™
with BLASTER RIFLE and PISTOL

COLLECTION 3

Captain Piett
3 3/4-inch POF with slide
$6 in package

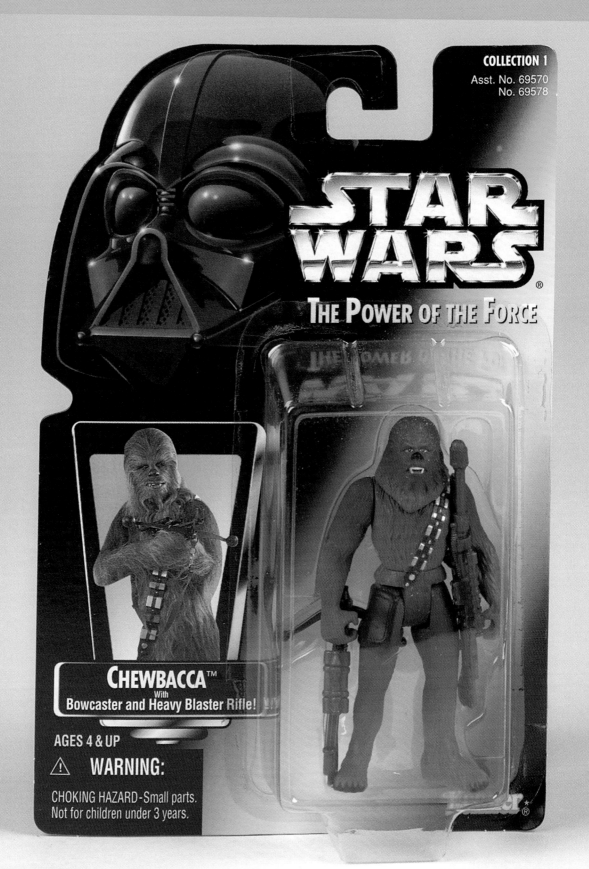

COLLECTION 1
Asst. No. 69570
No. 69578

STAR WARS®

THE POWER OF THE FORCE

CHEWBACCA™
With
Bowcaster and Heavy Blaster Rifle!

AGES 4 & UP

⚠ **WARNING:**

CHOKING HAZARD–Small parts.
Not for children under 3 years.

Chewbacca
3 3/4-inch Power of the Force
$4 loose, $10 in package

SPECIAL LIMITED EDITION!

Asst. No. 69675
No. 84023

STAR WARS
THE POWER OF THE FORCE

CHEWBACCA™

AGES 4 AND UP

⚠ **WARNING:**
CHOKING HAZARD-Small parts.
Not for children under 3 years.

Chewbacca
3 3/4-inch Millennium Mint
$25 in package

Malakili 2

Nien Numb 2

Ponda Baba. 2

Princess Leia. 2

Rebel Fleet Trooper 2

Rebel Fleet Trooper II. 2

Saelt-Marae. 2

Weequay 2

STAR WARS: POWER OF THE FORCE BEAST ASSORTMENT (1997-98)

Han Solo / Jabba (.00). 20

Han Solo / Jabba (.01). 10

Jawa / Ronto 10

Sandtrooper / Dewback 10

Tauntaun with Luke Skywalker . 10

STAR WARS: POWER OF THE FORCE ELECTRONIC POWER FX (1997)

Ben Kenobi 3

Darth Vader. 3

Emperor (.00) 4

Emperor (.01) 3

Luke Skywalker 3

R2-D2 3

STAR WARS: POWER OF THE

FORCE (EXCLUSIVES / MAIL-INS, 1997-98)

B'Omarr Monk. 10

Darth Vader with Obi Wan Kenobi. 50

Grand Moff Tarkin with Death Star Gunner 12-inch 65

Han Solo Stormtrooper 15

Luke Skywalker:

Theatre Edition 40

Sandtrooper 12-inch 30

Spirit of Obi Wan Kenobi 10

STAR WARS: POWER OF THE FORCE (1998)

Ben Kenobi (.00) 2

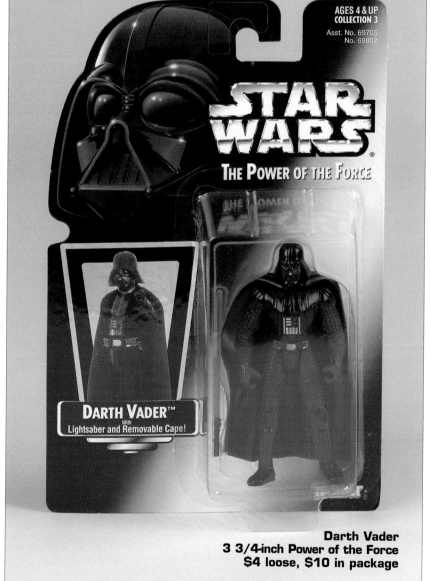

Darth Vader
3 3/4-inch Power of the Force
$4 loose, $10 in package

THE **Kenner** COLLECTION™

STAR WARS®

THE POWER OF THE FORCE

FREEZE FRAME™ ACTION SLIDE
ACTUAL MOVIE SCENES To See & Project

STAR WARS®

ROJ

DARTH VADER™
Luke Skywalker removes Vader's mask to reveal Anakin Skywalker.

Works with standard slide projector.

⚠ **WARNING:**
CHOKING HAZARD–Small parts. Not for children under 3 years.

AGES 4 & UP

Asst.

WITH DETACHABLE HAND

DARTH VADER™
WITH REMOVABLE HELMET AND LIGHTSABER

COLLECTION 3

Darth Vader
3 3/4-inch POF with slide
$6 in package

COLLECTION 1
Asst. No. 69570
No. 69608

STAR WARS ®

THE POWER OF THE FORCE

DEATH STAR GUNNER™
with
RADIATION SUIT AND BLASTER PISTOL

AGES 4 & UP

⚠ **WARNING:**

CHOKING HAZARD–Small parts.
Not for children under 3 years.

Kenner ®

**Death Star Gunner
3 3/4-inch Power of the Force
$8 loose, $20 in package**

AGES 4 & UP

Asst. No. 69610
No. 69677

⚠ **WARNING:**
CHOKING HAZARD-Small parts.
Not for children under 3 years.

STAR WARS™

DELUXE
PROBE DROID™
With PROTON TORPEDO AND SELF-DESTRUCT EXPLODING HEAD

GALACTIC EMPIRE

Probe Droid
Power of the Force Deluxe pack
$4 loose, $10 in package

Ben Kenobi (.01) 2

Endor Rebel Soldier (.00) 2

Endor Rebel Soldier (.01) 2

Han Solo Bespin (.00) 2

Han Solo Bespin (.01) 2

Han Solo Carbonite (.00) 2

Han Solo Carbonite (.01) 2

Han Solo Endor (.00) 2

Han Solo Endor (.01) 2

Hoth Rebel Soldier (.00) 2

Hoth Rebel Soldier (.01) 2

Lando Calrissian (.00) 2

Lando Calrissian (.01) 2

Lando Calrissian Skiff (.00) 2

Lando Calrissian Skiff (.01) 2

Princess Leia Ewok Gear (.00) . . 2

Princess Leia Ewok Gear (.01) . . 2

Princess Leia Jabba's Prisoner

(.00) 2

Princess Leia Jabba's Prisoner

(.01) 2

Luke Skywalker Bespin (.00) . . . 2

Luke Skywalker Bespin (.01) . . . 2

Luke Skywalker Stormtrooper

(.00) 2

Luke Skywalker Stormtrooper

(.01) 2

Rebel Fleet Trooper (.00) 2

Rebel Fleet Trooper (.01) 2

STAR WARS EPIC FORCE (1998)

Boba Fett 6

C-3PO 6

Darth Vader 6

Luke Skywalker 6

STAR WARS MILLENIUM MINT

Han Solo in Bespin Fatigues 5

Chewbacca (with coin) 5

Snowtrooper (with coin) 5

STAR WARS PRINCESS LEIA

COLLECTION (1998)

Princess Leia / Luke Skywalker

(.00) 6

Princess Leia / Luke Skywalker

(.01) 6

Princess Leia / Han Solo (.00) . . 6

Princess Leia / Han Solo (.01) . . 6

Princess Leia / Wicket (.00) 6

Princess Leia / Wicket (.01) 6

Princess Leia / R2-D2 (.00) 6

Princess Leia / R2-D2 (.01) 6

Emperor Palpatine 3 3/4-inch POF with slide $12in package

THE **Kenner** COLLECTION ™

STAR WARS®

THE POWER OF THE FORCE

FREEZE FRAME™
ACTION SLIDE
ACTUAL MOVIE SCENES
TO SEE & PROJECT

STAR WARS®

EMPEROR'S ROYAL GUARD™
Emperor Palpatine's elite personal guards.

Works with standard slide projector

EMPEROR'S ROYAL GUARD™
with FORCE PIKE

AGES 4 & UP

**Emperor's Royal Guard
3 3/4-inch POF with slide
$8 in package**

THE **Kenner** COLLECTION ™

STAR WARS®

THE POWER OF THE FORCE

FREEZE FRAME™ ACTION SLIDE
ACTUAL MOVIE SCENES To SEE & PROJECT

STAR WARS®

ENDOR™ REBEL SOLDIER
The mission on Endor's forest moon goes temporarily awry

Works with standard slide projector

⚠ **WARNING:**

CHOKING HAZARD–Small parts.
Not for children under 3 years.

AGES 4 & UP

ENDOR™ REBEL SOLDIER
with SURVIVAL BACKPACK and BLASTER RIFLE

Endor Rebel Soldier
3 3/4-inch POF with slide
$6 in package

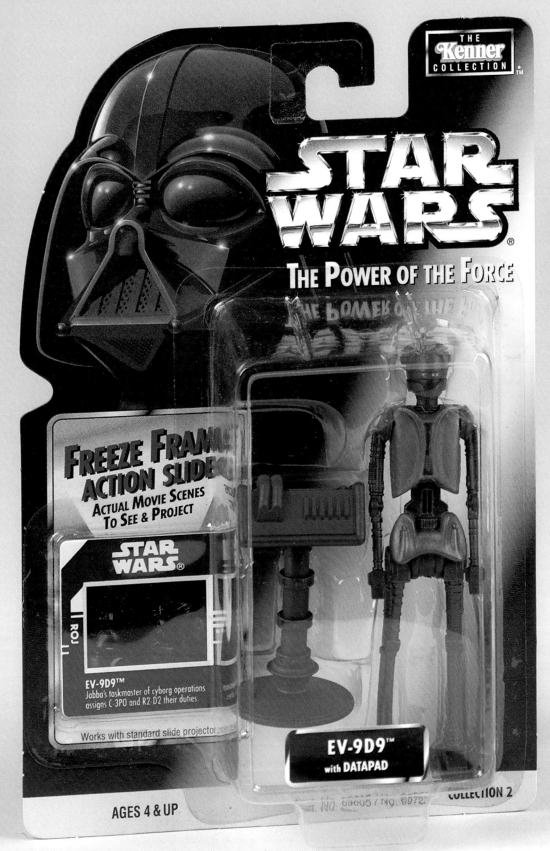

THE
Kenner
COLLECTION™

STAR WARS®

THE POWER OF THE FORCE

FREEZE FRAME ACTION SLIDE
ACTUAL MOVIE SCENES
TO SEE & PROJECT

STAR WARS®

EV-9D9™
Jabba's taskmaster of cyborg operations
assigns C-3PO and R2-D2 their duties.

Works with standard slide projector

EV-9D9™
with DATAPAD

COLLECTION 2

AGES 4 & UP

EV-9D9
3 3/4-inch POF with slide
$6 in package

CARDED FIGURES

STAR WARS: POWER OF THE FORCE (1995)

Ben Kenobi (half shot, long lightsaber). 50

Ben Kenobi (full shot, long lightsaber). 50

Ben Kenobi (full shot, short lightsaber). 10

Chewbacca 10

C-3PO. 10

Darth Vader (long lightsaber) 30

Darth Vader (short lightsaber). 10

Darth Vader(short lightsaber, long pack) 20

Han Solo 10

Luke Skywalker (long lightsaber) 40

Luke Skywalker (short lightsaber). 15

Princess Leia (two bands) 15

Princess Leia (three bands) . . . 20

R2-D2. 10

Stormtrooper. 12

STAR WARS: POWER OF THE FORCE (1996)

Boba Fett (circle on hand) 10

Boba Fett (half-circle on hand) . 70

Chewbacca 10

Dash Rendar 6

Death Star Gunner (green). . . . 10

Death Star Gunner (red). 20

Greedo (green) 6

Greedo (red) 20

Hammerhead (green). 6

Hammerhead (red) 20

Han Solo (in carbonite) 6

Han Solo (in carbonite and freeze chamber). 12

Han Solo (Hoth open hand) . . . 20

Han Solo (Hoth closed hand) . . 10

Jawa (red). 20

Jawa (green) 8

Lando Calrissian 6

Luke Skywalker (long lightsaber) 25

Luke Skywalker (short lightsaber). 10

Luke Skywalker (short lightsaber, long pack) . . 15

Ewoks: Wicket & Logray
3 3/4-inch POF with slide
$12 in package

Grand Moff Tarkin
3 3/4-inch Power of the Force
$2 loose, $6 in package

COLLECTION 1
Asst. No. 69570
No. 69606

STAR WARS®

THE POWER OF THE FORCE

GREEDO™
with
BLASTER PISTOL

AGES 4 & UP

⚠ WARNING:

CHOKING HAZARD-Small parts.
Not for children under 3 years.

kenner®

Greedo
3 3/4-inch Power of the Force
$2 loose, $6 in package

COLLECTION 1
Asst. No. 69570
No. 69577

STAR WARS®

THE POWER OF THE FORCE

HAN SOLO™
With
Heavy Assault Rifle and Blaster!

AGES 4 & UP

⚠ **WARNING:**

CHOKING HAZARD–Small parts.
Not for children under 3 years.

Han Solo
3 3/4-inch Power of the Force
$4 loose, $10 in package

Luke Skywalker: Jedi Knight
(brown vest) 60

Luke Skywalker: Jedi Knight
(black vest) 6

Luke Skywalker in Dagobah
Fatigues (short light saber) 6

Luke Skywalker in Dagobah
Fatigues (long light saber) 30

Luke Skywalker:
Stormtrooper (red) 20

Luke Skywalker: Stormtrooper
(green) 10

Luke Skywalker: X-Wing Pilot (long
lightsaber) 25

Luke Skywalker: X-Wing Pilot
(short lightsaber) 10

Luke Skywalker: X-Wing Pilot
(short saber, long pack) 25

Prince Xizor 6

Princess Leia in Boussh Disguise 6

R5-D4 (red) 20

R5-D4 (green, straight latch) . . 20

R5-D4 (green, hook latch) 6

Sandtrooper 10

Tatooine Stormtrooper 20

Tie Fighter (without sticker) 6

Tie Fighter (with sticker) 25

Tusken Raider (closed, green) . 30

Tusken Raider (open, green) . . . 6

Tusken Raider (closed, red) . . . 20

Tusken Raider (open, red) 20

Yoda 10

STAR WARS: POWER OF THE FORCE (TWO-PACKS AND THREE-PACKS, 1996-97)

Ben Kenobi / Darth Vader /
Luke Skywalker 40

Boba Fett / IG-88 40

Chewbacca / Han Solo /
Lando Calrissian 40

C-3PO / R2-D2 /

Stormtrooper 40

Luke Skywalker / Tusken Raider /
Ben Kenobi 40

Luke Skywalker / Lando Calrissian
/ Tie Fighter 40

Luke Skywalker / AT-ST Driver /
Princess Leia 40

Xizor / Darth Vader 40

STAR WARS: POWER OF THE

COLLECTION 2
Asst. No. 69605
No. 69613

**Han Solo In Carbonite
3 3/4-inch Power of the Force
$2 loose, $6 in package**

COLLECTION 1
Asst. No. 69570
No. 69621

STAR WARS®

THE POWER OF THE FORCE

HAN SOLO™ IN ENDOR GEAR
with
BLASTER PISTOL

AGES 4 & UP

⚠ **WARNING:**

CHOKING HAZARD-Small parts.
Not for children under 3 years.

Han Solo In Endor Gear
3 3/4-inch Power of the Force
$2 loose, $6 in package

FORCE BEAST ASSORTMENT (1997-98)

Han Solo / Jabba (.00) 40
Han Solo / Jabba (.01) 20
Jawa / Ronto 20
Sandtrooper / Dewback 20
Tauntaun with
Luke Skywalker 20

STAR WARS: POWER OF THE FORCE ELECTRONIC POWER FX (1997)

Ben Kenobi 8
Darth Vader 8
Emperor (.00) 10
Emperor (.01) 8
Luke Skywalker 8
R2-D2 8

STAR WARS: POWER OF THE FORCE (EXCLUSIVES / MAIL-INS, 1997-98)

B'Omarr Monk 20
Darth Vader with
Obi Wan Kenobi 100
Grand Moff Tarkin with Death Star
Gunner 12-inch 125
Greedo 12-inch 60
Han Solo Stormtrooper 30

Luke Skywalker:
Theatre Edition 100
Sandtrooper 12-inch 75
Spirit of Obi Wan Kenobi 15

STAR WARS: POWER OF THE FORCE (1998)

Ben Kenobi (.00) 15
Ben Kenobi (.01) 6
Endor Rebel Soldier (.00) 15
Endor Rebel Soldier (.01) 6

Han Solo Bespin (.00) 30
Han Solo Bespin (.01) 6
Han Solo Carbonite (.00) 15
Han Solo Carbonite (.01) 6
Han Solo Endor (.00) 15
Han Solo Endor (.01) 6
Hoth Rebel Soldier (.00) 15
Hoth Rebel Soldier (.01) 6
Lando Calrissian (.00) 15
Lando Calrissian (.01) 6
Lando Calrissian Skiff (.00) . . . 15
Lando Calrissian Skiff (.01) 6

**Hoth Rebel Soldier
3 3/4-inch Power of the Force
$2 loose, $6 in package**

Ishi Tib
3 3/4-inch POF with slide
$12 in package

COLLECTION 2
Asst. No. 69605
No. 69607

STAR WARS®

THE POWER OF THE FORCE

JAWAS™
with
GLOWING EYES AND IONIZATION BLASTERS

AGES 4 & UP

⚠ WARNING:

CHOKING HAZARD–Small parts.
Not for children under 3 years.

Kenner®

Jawas
3 3/4-inch Power of the Force
$8 loose, $20 in package

THE **Kenner** COLLECTION ™

STAR WARS®

THE POWER OF THE FORCE

FREEZE FRAME™
ACTION SLIDE
ACTUAL MOVIE SCENES
TO SEE & PROJECT

STAR WARS®

SW

LAK SIVRAK™
Doing business in Mos Eisley Spaceport's
infamous cantina.

Works with standard slide projector

⚠ **WARNING:**
CHOKING HAZARD-Small parts.
Not for children under 3 years.

AGES
4 & UP

LAK SIVRAK™
with BLASTER PISTOL
and VIBRO-BLADE

Asst. 69607 NO. 69753

COLLECTION 2

Lak Sivrak
3 3/4-inch POF with slide
$12 in package

Princess Leia Ewok Gear (.00) . 15

Princess Leia Ewok Gear (.01) . . 6

Princess Leia Jabba's Prisoner
(.00) 15

Princess Leia Jabba's Prisoner
(.01) 6

Luke Skywalker Bespin (.00) . . 30

Luke Skywalker Bespin (.01) . . 15

Luke Skywalker Stormtrooper
(.00) 15

Luke Skywalker Stormtrooper
(.01) 3

Rebel Fleet Trooper (.00) 15

Rebel Fleet Trooper (.01) 6

STAR WARS EPIC FORCE (1998)

Boba Fett. 15

C-3PO 15

Darth Vader. 15

Luke Skywalker 15

STAR WARS MILLENIUM MINT

Han Solo in Bespin Fatigues with
coin (with text) 25

Han Solo in Bespin Fatigues
with coin (no text) 20

Chewbacca with coin
(with text) 25

Chewbacca with coin
(no text) 20

Snowtrooper with coin

(with text) 25

Snowtrooper with coin
(no text) 20

Luke Skywalker in Endor Gear
with coin 20

Princess Leia in Endor Gear
with coin 20

Emperor Palpatine with coin . . 20

C-3PO with coin 20

STAR WARS PRINCESS LEIA

COLLECTION (1998)

Princess Leia / Luke Skywalker
(.00) 20

Princess Leia / Luke Skywalker
(.01) 15

Princess Leia / Han Solo (.00) . 20

Princess Leia / Han Solo (.01) . 15

Princess Leia / Wickett (.00) . . 20

Princess Leia / Wickett (.01) . . 15

Princess Leia / R2-D2 (.00) . . . 20

Princess Leia / R2-D2 (.01) . . . 15

**Lando Calrissian 3 3/4-inch
Power of the Force
$2 loose, $6 in package**

THE Kenner COLLECTION ™

STAR WARS®
THE POWER OF THE FORCE

FREEZE FRAME™ ACTION SLIDE
ACTUAL MOVIE SCENES TO SEE & PROJECT

STAR WARS®

ROJ

LANDO CALRISSIAN™
Lando is appointed general to lead the Rebel assault on the second Death Star.

Works with standard slide projector

⚠ **WARNING:**
CHOKING HAZARD—Small parts.
Not for children under 3 years.

AGES 4 & UP

Asst

COLLECTION 1

LANDO CALRISSIAN™
in GENERAL'S GEAR
with BLASTER PISTOL

Lando Calrissian
3 3/4-inch POF with slide
$12 in package

COLLECTION 1
Asst. No. 69570
No. 69818

STAR WARS®

THE POWER OF THE FORCE

LEIA™ IN BOUSHH DISGUISE
with
BLASTER RIFLE AND BOUNTY HUNTER HELMET

AGES 4 & UP

⚠ **WARNING:**

CHOKING HAZARD-Small parts.
Not for children under 3 years.

Kenner®

Leia in Boush Disguise
3 3/4-inch Power of the Force
$2 loose, $6 in package

Asst. No. 69570
No. 69571

STAR WARS

THE POWER OF THE FORCE

LUKE SKYWALKER™
With
Grappling-Hook Blaster and Lightsaber!

AGES 4 & UP

⚠ **WARNING:**

CHOKING HAZARD-Small parts.
Not for children under 3 years.

Luke Skywalker
3 3/4-inch Power of the Force
$15 loose, $40 in package

(with text) 25

Snowtrooper with coin

(no text) 20

Luke Skywalker in Endor Gear

with coin 20

Princess Leia in Endor Gear

with coin 20

Emperor Palpatine with coin . . 20

C-3PO with coin 20

STAR WARS PRINCESS LEIA COLLECTION (1998)

Princess Leia / Luke Skywalker

(.00) 20

Princess Leia / Luke Skywalker

(.01) 15

Princess Leia / Han Solo (.00) . 20

Princess Leia / Han Solo (.01) . 15

Princess Leia / Wickett (.00) . . 20

Princess Leia / Wickett (.01) . . 15

Princess Leia / R2-D2 (.00) . . . 20

Princess Leia / R2-D2 (.01) . . . 15

FIGURES WITH ACTION SLIDES

Admiral Ackbar 6

AT-ST Driver 6

Ben Kenobi (.03) 12

Ben Kenobi (.04) 6

Bespin Luke Skywalker 12

Biggs Darklighter 6

Boba Fett 10

Captain Piett 6

Darth Vader 6

Emperor Palpatine 6

Emperor's Royal Guard 8

Endor Rebel Soldier 6

EV-9D9 6

Ewoks: Wicket and Logray 12

Gamorrean Guard 6

Garindan (with long snoot) . . . 10

Grand Moff Tarkin 6

Han Solo in Bespin Gear (.01) . 12

Han Solo in Bespin Gear (.02) . . 6

Han Solo in Carbonite (.04) . . . 12

Han Solo in Carbonite (.05) 6

Han Solo in Endor Gear (.01) . . 12

Han Solo in Endor Gear (.02) . . . 6

Hoth Rebel Soldier (.01) 12

Hoth Rebel Soldier (.02) 6

Hoth Snowtrooper 10

Ishi Tib 12

Lando Calrissian as

Skiff Guard (.01) 12

Lando Clarissian as

Skiff Guard (.02) 6

Luke Skywalker In Ceremonial Outfit
3 3/4-inch Power of the Force
$2 loose, $6 in package

Asst. No. 69570
No. 69588

STAR WARS®

THE POWER OF THE FORCE

LUKE SKYWALKER™
in DAGOBAH FATIGUES
With Lightsaber and Blaster Pistol!

AGES 4 & UP

⚠ **WARNING:**

CHOKING HAZARD—Small parts.
Not for children under 3 years.

Luke Skywalker in Dagobah Fatigues
3 3/4-inch Power of the Force
$2 loose, $5 in package

COLLECTION 2
Asst. No. 69605
No. 69619

STAR WARS®

THE POWER OF THE FORCE

LUKE SKYWALKER™ IN HOTH GEAR
with
BLASTER PISTOL AND LIGHTSABER

AGES 4 & UP

⚠ WARNING:

CHOKING HAZARD—Small parts.
Not for children under 3 years.

Luke Skywalker In Hoth Gear
3 3/4-inch Power of the Force
$2 loose, $10 in package

COLLECTION 2
Asst. No. 69605
No. 69604

STAR WARS®

THE POWER OF THE FORCE

LUKE SKYWALKER™
IN STORMTROOPER™ DISGUISE
with
IMPERIAL ISSUE BLASTER

AGES 4 & UP

⚠ WARNING:

CHOKING HAZARD-Small parts.
Not for children under 3 years.

**Luke Skywalker In
Stormtrooper Disguise
3 3/4-inch Power of the Force
$8 loose, $20 in package**

Leia as Jabba Dancer (.01). . . . 12

Leia as Jabba Dancer (.02) 6

Lando Calrissian 12

Luke Skywalker in Stormtrooper
Disguise (.03) 12

Luke Skywalker in Stormtrooper
Disguise (.04) 6

Malakili the Rancor Keeper. 6

Nien Numb 6

Rebel Fleet Trooper (.01) 12

Rebel Fleet Trooper (.02) 6

Saelt-Marae the Yak Face. 6

Stormtrooper. 6

Tie Fighter Pilot 6

Weequay 10

OTHERS

C-3PO (green tint, red card, from
Japan). 30

C-3PO (green tint, green card,
from Japan). 20

Cantina Band Member (Fan Club
mail-in exclusive). 20

Darktrooper (from "Dark Forces"
video game) 6

Imperial Probe Droid Deluxe
Figure (orange on back). 50

Spacetrooper (from the novel
"Heir to the Empire") 6

Spirit of Obi-Wan Kenobi (Frito-
Lay mail-in exclusive) 15

12-INCH FIGURES

STAR WARS: POWER OF THE FORCE

	Loose	MIB
Admiral Ackbar.	15	30
AT-AT Driver.	30	60
Ben Kenobi.	30	60
Boba Fett	30	60
Ceremonial Luke		
Skywalker.	35	70
Chewbacca.	25	50
C-3PO	15	30
Darth Vader	20	40
Grand Moff Tarkin. . .	15	30
Greedo.	30	60
Han Solo	20	40
Han Solo in		
Hoth Gear.	20	40
Jawa	10	20
Lando Calrissian. . . .	15	30
Luke Skywalker	20	40

Asst. No. 69570
No. 69581

LUKE SKYWALKER
in X-wing Fighter Pilot Gear
With Lightsaber and Blaster Pistol!

AGES 4 & UP
⚠ **WARNING:**
CHOKING HAZARD–Small parts.
Not for children under 3 years.

**Luke Skywalker: X-Wing Pilot
3 3/4-inch Power of the Force
$10 loose, $25 in package**

Asst. No. 69605
No. 69596

AGES 4 & UP

STAR WARS®

THE POWER OF THE FORCE

JEDI KNIGHT
LUKE SKYWALKER™
with
LIGHTSABER AND REMOVABLE CLOAK

Luke Skywalker: Jedi Knight
3 3/4-inch Power of the Force
$25 loose, $60 in package

No. 69794

STAR WARS ®

THE POWER OF THE FORCE

SPECIAL
THE
STAR
WARS
TRILOGY
EDITION

LUKE SKYWALKER
JEDI KNIGHT
THEATER EDITION

Return of The Jedi Special Edition • Opening Day • March 7, 1997

Kenner®

Luke Skywalker: Jedi Knight
3 3/4-inch POF Special Edition
$40 loose, $100 in package

AGES 4 & UP
COLLECTION 1

Asst. No. 69570
No. 69574

STAR WARS®

THE POWER OF THE FORCE

R2-D2™
With
Light-Pipe Eye Port and Retractable Leg!

Kenner®

R2-D2
3 3/4-inch Power of the Force
$4 loose, $10 in package

Luke Skywalker in
Bespin Fatigues . . . . 20. . 40Luke

Luke Skywalker in
Hoth Battle Gear. . . . 15 35

Luke Skywalker:

X-Wing Pilot. 15 35

Princess Leia 15 35

R2-D2 . . . . 10 20

Sandtrooper. 25 50

Snowtrooper 25 50

Stormtrooper 15 30

Tie Fighter Pilot 15 30

Tusken Raider
(with blaster) 15 35

Tusken Raider with
Gaderffii Stick. 15 35

Yoda 10 20

EXCLUSIVES

AT-AT Driver (from Service
Merchandise). 75

Cantina Band, complete set
(Wal-Mart). 300

Doikk Na'ts from Cantina Band
(Wal-Mart). 40

Figrin D'an from Cantina Band
(Wal-Mart). 60

Ickabel from Cantina Band
(Wal-Mart). 40

Nalan from Cantina Band
(Wal-Mart). 40

Tech from Cantina Band
(Wal-Mart). 40

Tedn from Cantina Band
(Wal-Mart). 40

Electronic Ben Kenobi vs.
Darth Vader (J.C. Penney) . . . 100

Greedo (J.C. Penney). 50

Han and Taun-Taun

(Toys "R" Us) 120

Luke Skywalker and Han Solo,
stormtrooper disguise
(KayBee) 125

Luke Skywalker and Wampa
(Target) 125

Luke Skywalker: Jedi Knight and
Bib Fortuna (FAO Schwartz) . . 150

COLLECTION 1
Asst. No. 69570
No. 69579

STAR WARS

THE POWER OF THE FORCE

PRINCESS LEIA ORGANA
with
"Laser" Pistol and Assault Rifle!

AGES 4 & UP

⚠ WARNING:
CHOKING HAZARD–Small parts.
Not for children under 3 years.

**Princess Leia Organa
3 3/4-inch Power of the Force
$2 loose, $10 in package**

Princess Leia Organa as
Jabba's Prisoner
3 3/4-inch POF with slide
$6 in package

Dept. 07
WAL-MART
$19.96

FULLY
POSEABLE!

STAR
WARS

AGES 4 & UP
27904/27903 Asst.

GREEDO™

**Greedo
12-inch
$30 loose, $60 in package**

Han Solo in Hoth Gear
12-inch
$20 loose, $60 in package

STAR WARS
ACTION COLLECTION

FIRING REBEL
BLASTER
INCLUDED!

STAR
WARS™

CAUTION: Do not aim
weapons at eyes or face.

AGES 4 & UP
27917/27915 Asst.

LUKE SKYWALKER™
In Hoth Gear

⚠ WARNING:
CHOKING HAZARD-Small parts.
Not for children under 3 years.

Luke Skywalker in Hoth Gear
12-inch
$15 loose, $35 in package

IMPERIAL DROID INCLUDED!

STAR WARS™

SANDTROOPER

AGES 4 & UP
27906/27903 Asst.

Sandtrooper
12-inch
$25 loose, $50 in package

Snowtrooper
12-inch
$15 loose, $30 in package

**Grand Moff Tarkin & Imperial
Gunnder 12-inch
$125 loose, $175 in package**

HAN SOLO™ & LUKE SKYWALKER™
In Stormtrooper Gear

Han Solo and Luke Skywalker
12-inch
$125 loose, $175 in package

Luke Skywalker Vs. Wampa
12-inch
$125 loose, $175 in package

A-Wing Fighter
Power of the Force Vehicle
$10 loose, $25 in package

VEHICLES PLAY SETS ACCESSORIES DIE CASTS & PRICE GUIDE

If it flies, walks, speeds or crawls, there's a toy for it. A-Wings, AT-ATs and Air Speeders are all represented in the vintage and new lines of Star Wars-related accesories.

Kenner released numerous Star Wars vehicles when the movies first came out, then released another series of vehicles with the new Power of the Force line.

Most of the newer items are very similar to the older ones. They've adjusted some of the color schemes so that what was a solid gray or white color before now has a little more detail such as battle-damaged scars and marks. Otherwise, the ships are virtually the same.

Vehicle collecting is not as popular as action figure collecting. The older vehicles are more collectible, since you can still go to toy stores today and find the new vehicles. A lot of the cooler ships were made in the '70s and '80s. Some of the more popular vintage vehicles include the Radio-Controlled Jawa Sandcrawler from "Star Wars," a fairly expensive and rare piece that was really well done.

There are a lot of nice vehicles from the original Return of the Jedi collection, including the Imperial Shuttle. Another piece that is real popular, but also real rare, is the Tatooine Skiff, which was included in the 1984 Power of the Force series. The Skiff depicted the scene from "Return of the Jedi" with Luke Skywalker and the Sarlaac Pit. Another hot vehicle is the Y-Wing Fighter, which wasn't released until the Return of the Jedi set, despite the vehicle's inclusion in "Star Wars."

In addition to the large vehicles, which were designed to incorporate the 3 3/4-inch action figures, there was also a set of smaller die-cast vehicles, although they tend to not be as popular among collectors. Die-cast collectors tend to be a

A-Wing Fighter (above)
Vintage Star Wars Vehicle
$150 loose, $500 in package
Darth Vader's Tie Fighter (left)
Power of the Force Vehicle
$12 loose, $30 in package

AT-AT
Vintage Star Wars Vehicle
$125 loose, $200 in package

unique bunch: not many people who collect the action figures collect the die-cast, and vice versa. In general, the die-cast items are fairly inexpensive, so it could provide an affordable entry into the hobby for the more budget-conscious collector.

By far the most desirable die-cast item is the Tie Bomber, which was a very limited release and was never offered in the larger format. The Bomber goes for about $300 out of the package and anywhere from $600 to $1,500 in the package.

In addition to the larger plastic vehicles and the medium-sized die-casts, there was also a Micro Collection, a group of 1-inch die-cast metal figures that represented ships and machines from the films. The pieces are fairly well done and are somewhat popular among collectors, although they still aren't as sought after as the large-scale items.

VEHICLES, PLAY SETS, ACCESSORIES AND DIE-CAST (1977-PRESENT)

(Prices for packaged items indicate items in their originally issued packaging. Prices are for opened boxes with unused contents.)

VEHICLES (1978-85)

STAR WARS ACCESORIES

	Loose	MIB
AT-AT	125	200
AT-ST	35	75
A-Wing Fighter	150	500
Battle Damaged TIE Fighter	40	100
Battle Damaged X-Wing Fighter	40	150
B-Wing Fighter	100	200
Cloud Car	30	125
Darth Vader TIE Fighter	60	150
Imperial Cruiser (Sears exclusive)	40	125
Imperial Shuttle	225	400

Imperial Troop Transport	40	125
Landspeeder	20	80
Millennium Falcon	75	200
Rebel Transport	50	125
Sandcrawler	325	600
Slave 1	50	200
Snowspeeder	40	100
Speeder Bike	15	40
Tatooine Skiff	400	700
TIE Fighter	40	200
TIE Interceptor	75	150
X-Wing Figher	40	150
Y-Wing Fighter	60	200

VEHICLES (1995-PRESENT)

STAR WARS POWER OF THE FORCE (ACCESSORIES, 1995-98)

A-Wing Fighter	10	25
Air Speeder	8	20
C-3PO Talking Case	8	20
Chewbacca Bowcaster	8	20
Cloud Car	8	20

Tie Interceptor Micro Machines Collection $6 loose, $10 in package

Star Destroyer
Power of the Force Vehicle
$8 loose, $30 in package

STAR DESTROYER™

Millennium Falcon
Power of the Force Vehicle
$20 loose, $50 in package

X-Wing Fighter
Power of the Force Vehicle
$10 loose, $30 in package

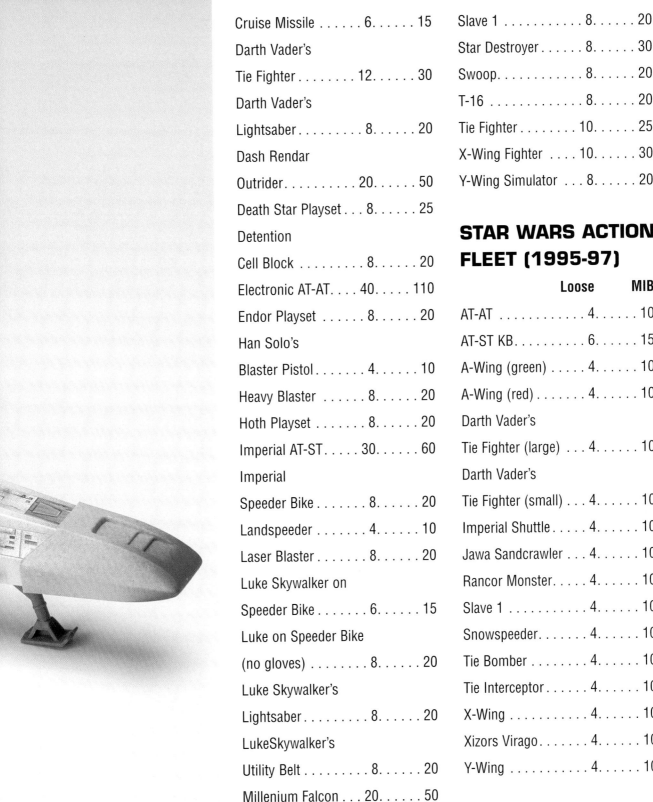

Cruise Missile 6 15

Darth Vader's

Tie Fighter 12 30

Darth Vader's

Lightsaber 8 20

Dash Rendar

Outrider 20 50

Death Star Playset . . . 8 25

Detention

Cell Block 8 20

Electronic AT-AT 40 110

Endor Playset 8 20

Han Solo's

Blaster Pistol 4 10

Heavy Blaster 8 20

Hoth Playset 8 20

Imperial AT-ST 30 60

Imperial

Speeder Bike 8 20

Landspeeder 4 10

Laser Blaster 8 20

Luke Skywalker on

Speeder Bike 6 15

Luke on Speeder Bike

(no gloves) 8 20

Luke Skywalker's

Lightsaber 8 20

LukeSkywalker's

Utility Belt 8 20

Millenium Falcon . . . 20 50

Rebel Blockade Runner8 20

Rebel Snowspeeder . . 8 20

Remote R2-D2 . . . . . . 8 20

Slave 1 . . . . 8 20

Star Destroyer 8 30

Swoop 8 20

T-16 . . . . 8 20

Tie Fighter 10 25

X-Wing Fighter 10 30

Y-Wing Simulator . . . 8 20

STAR WARS ACTION FLEET (1995-97)

	Loose	MIB
AT-AT	4	10
AT-ST KB	6	15
A-Wing (green)	4	10
A-Wing (red)	4	10
Darth Vader's Tie Fighter (large)	4	10
Darth Vader's Tie Fighter (small)	4	10
Imperial Shuttle	4	10
Jawa Sandcrawler	4	10
Rancor Monster	4	10
Slave 1	4	10
Snowspeeder	4	10
Tie Bomber	4	10
Tie Interceptor	4	10
X-Wing	4	10
Xizors Virago	4	10
Y-Wing	4	10

MICRO MACHINES

	Loose	MIB
AT-ST	6	10

A-Wing 6 10

B-Wing 6 10

Imperial Shuttle 6 10

Jabba's Sail Barge . . . 6 10

Rebel Transport 6 10

Star Destroyer 6 10

Tie Interceptor 6 10

DIE-CASTS (1978-85)

STAR WARS ACCESSORIES

	Loose	MIB
Cloud Car	20	60
Darth Vader	20	50
Landspeeder	15	60
Millennium Falcon	15	175
Slave I	25	100
Snowspeeder	20	75
Star Destroyer	30	175
TIE Bomber	300	800
TIE Fighter	20	60
X-Wing	15	60
Y-Wing	30	175

STAR WARS: THE EMPIRE STRIKES BACK MICRO SET (1980)

	Loose	MIB

A-Wing
Micro Machines Collection
$6 loose, $10 in package

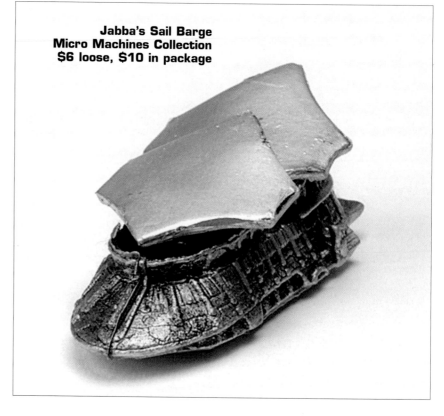

Jabba's Sail Barge
Micro Machines Collection
$6 loose, $10 in package

Imperial Shuttle
Vintage Star Wars Vehicle
$225 loose, $400 in package

Tie Fighter
Power of the Force Vehicle
$10 loose, **$25** in package

	Loose	MIB
Bespin Control Room.	20	40
Bespin Freeze Chamber	40	80
Bespin Gantry	20	40
Bespin World	90	175
Death Star Compactor	40	80
Death Star Escape	40	80
Death Star World	75	150
Hoth Generator Attack	15	30
Hoth Ion Cannon	15	30
Hoth Turret Defense	15	30
Hoth Wampa Cave	15	30
Hoth World	75	125
Millennium Falcon	200	400

	Loose	MIB
Snowspeeder	100	200
TIE Fighter	40	80
X-Wing	40	80

STAR WARS: THE EMPIRE STRIKES BACK MINI RIGS (1980)

	Loose	MIB
CAP-2	10	30
INT-4	10	30
MLC-3	10	30
MTV-7	10	30
PDT-8	10	30

STAR WARS: RETURN OF THE JEDI MINI RIGS

Millennium Falcon with case
Power of the Force Vehicle
$30 in package

(1983-84)

	Loose	MIB
AST-5	6	15
CAP-2	8	20
Desert Sail Skiff	6	15
Endor Forest Ranger	6	15
INT-4	8	20
ISP-6	10	30
MLC-3	8	20
MTV-7	10	30
PDT-8	8	20

STAR WARS: DROIDS CARTOON ACCESSORIES (1985)

	Loose	MIB
A-Wing Fighter	200	500
ATL Interceptor	20	50
Lightsaber	50	125
Sidegunner	20	50

STAR WARS: EWOKS CARTOONS (1985)

	Loose	MIB
Dulok Scout	8	20
Dulok Shaman	8	20
King Gorneesh	8	20
Lady Gorneesh	8	20
Logray	8	20
Wicket	12	30

Landspeeder
Vintage Star Wars Vehicle
$20 loose, $80 in package

Bespin Control Room
TESB Micro Set
$20 loose, $40 in package

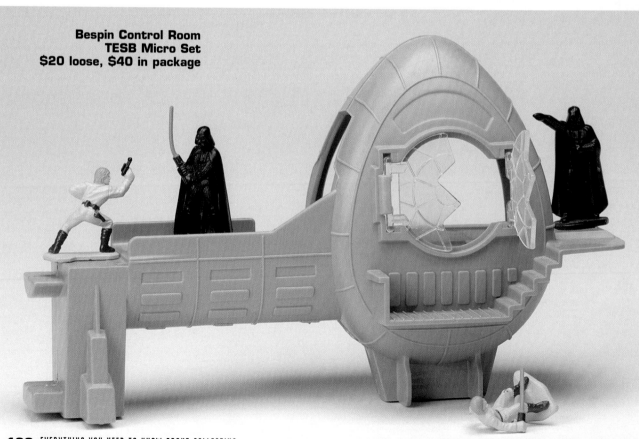

Slave 1
Power of the Force Vehicle
$8 loose, $20 in package

PLAY SETS (1978-85)

STAR WARS ACCESORIES

Cantina Adventure Set (Sears Exclusive, Includes four figures-Blue Snaggletooth, Greedo, Hammerhead and Walrusman) . . 300 600

Creature Cantina . . . 65 125

Cloud City (includes 4 figures-Han Bespin, Ugnaught, Dengar, and Lobot) 150 400

Dagobah 30 100

Darth Vader Star Destroyer 50 150

Death Star 100 300

Droid Factory 75 200

Ewok Village 80 175

Ice Planet Hoth 60 200

Land of the Jawas . . 75 150

Imperial Attack Base 30 100

Jabba the Hutt Throne Room 40 125

Jabba Dungeon (includes 3 figures- Klaatu Skiff, 8D8, and Nikto) 50 150

Jabba Dungeon (includes 3 figures- Amanaman, EV-9D9, and Barada) 200 350

Rebel Command Center (Sears exclusive, inlcudes Luke Hoth, R2-D2 with sensorscope, and AT-AT Commander) 80 200

Turret and Probot . . 50 150

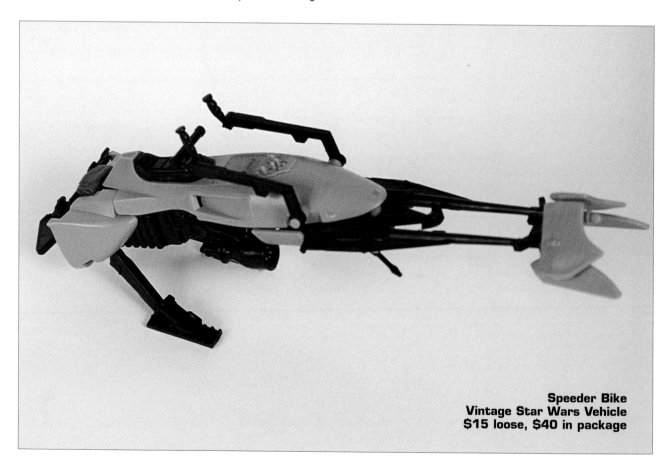

Speeder Bike
Vintage Star Wars Vehicle
$15 loose, $40 in package

Rebel Blockade Runner
Power of the Force Vehicle
$8 loose, $20 in package

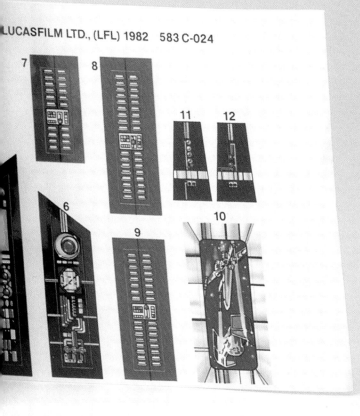

LUCASFILM LTD., (LFL) 1982   583 C-024

Death Star World
TESB Micro Set
$75 loose, $150 in package

Star Destroyer, AT-ST, Transport
Micro Machines Collection
$6 loose, $10 in package (each)

CREATURES

	Loose	MIB
Patrol Dewback	20	100
Rancor	50	100
Sy Snootles and Max Rebo Band	125	200
Taun-Taun (open belly)	40	125
Taun-Taun (solid belly)	25	80
Wampa	25	60

ACTION FIGURE CASES

	Loose	MIB
C-3PO Case	20	40
Chewbacca Bandolier Strap	5	20
Darth Vader Case	10	30
Empire Strikes Back Vinyl Case (Yoda on upper right corner)	30	50
Empire Strikes Back Vinyl Case (Wampa on upper right corner)	35	60
Laser Rifle Carry Case	15	50
Return of the Jedi Vinyl Case	75	150
Star Wars Vinyl Case	15	35

Max Rebo Band Micro Collection $15 loose, $30 in package

PLAY SETS (1995-PRESENT)

STAR WARS ACTION FLEET PLAY SETS (1995-97)

	Loose	MIB
Death Star	15	30
Hoth	15	30
Rebel Base	15	30

STAR WARS CINEMA SCENES (1997)

	Loose	MIB
Death Star Escape	6	15
Cantina Show Down	6	15
Jedi Final Dual (.00)	6	15
Jedi Final Dual (.01)	6	15
Pruchase of the Droids	6	15

STAR WARS BATTLE PACKS (1995-97)

	Loose	MIB
Alien / Creatures	4	10
Galactic Empire	4	10
Imperial Hunters	4	10
Rebel Alliance	4	10
Shadows of the Empire	4	10
Cantina	4	10
Desert Palace	4	10
Droid Escape	4	10
Dune Sea	4	10
Endor Ambassador	4	10
Mos Eisley	4	10

X-Wing with background
TESB Micro Set
$40 loose, $80 in package

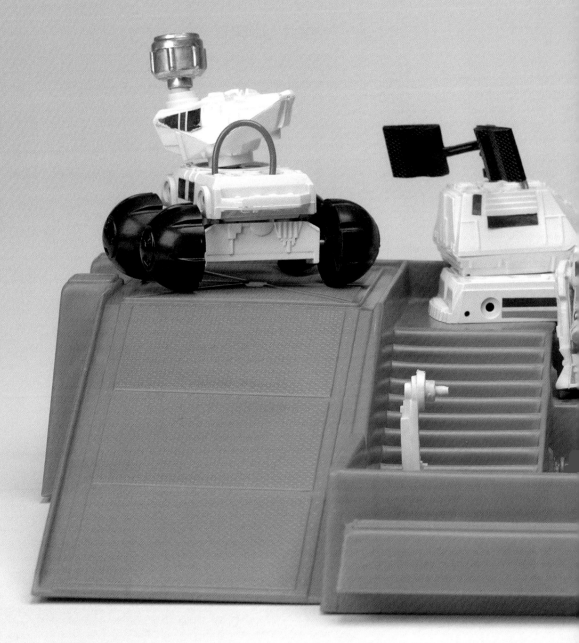

Droid Factory
Vintage Star Wars Play Set
$75 loose, $200 in package

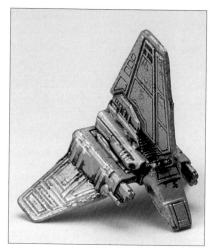

B-Wing, Imperial Shuttle
Micro Machines Collection
$6 loose, $10 in package (each)

Hoth Ice Planet Adventure Set
Vintage Star Wars Play Set
$55 loose, $150 in package

**Hoth Ice Planet
Vintage Star Wars Play Set
$60 loose, $200 in package**

**Tatooine Skiff
Vintage Star Wars Vehicle
$400 loose, $700 in package**

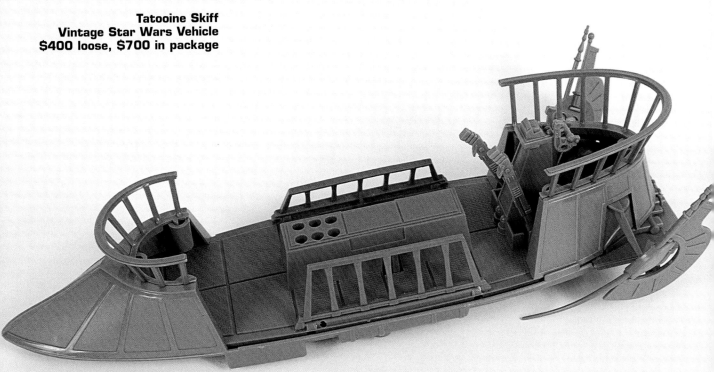

Tie Interceptor
Vintage Star Wars Vehicle
$75 loose, $150 in package

Rebel Snowspeeder
Power of the Force Vehicle
$8 loose, $20 in package

AT-ST
Vintage Star Wars Vehicle
$35 loose, $75 in package

Ceramic Yoda

EVERYTHING ELSE & CHECKLIST

You name it, and there's a Star Wars collectible: cookie jars, alarm clocks, bookmarks, drinking glasses and trading cards. And that's just the beginning.

ny toy-related Star Wars item is popular these days and is sure to be sought after by a collector somewhere. In fact, even the cardboard display used in stores to sell the first 12 figures is a hot item, now selling for close to $1,000. But there are thousands of non-toy items out there as well that make nice collectibles.

One of the first places to start is printed materials. There have been literally hundreds of publications related to "Star Wars." From comic books to science fiction magazines to posters, a collector could fill plenty of rooms with nothing but printed items.

Some of the most popular books are the original three novels, especially "Star Wars: From the Adventures of Luke Skywalker" by George Lucas, which appeared as a softcover novel nine months before "Star Wars" hit theaters. "The Empire Strikes Back" novel was written by Donald F. Glut, and "Return of the Jedi" was written by James Kahn.

The success of the films prompted the release of multiple Star Wars-related science fiction novels, most of which followed the adventures of the original characters to new and different places. In fact, the middle part of the '90s was a fertile time for Star Wars novels, especially Timothy Zahn's "Heir to the Empire" trilogy that followed the characters after the events of "Return of the Jedi."

In addition to novels, the Star Wars universe has been expanded upon in coloring books, activity books, information books and just about everything else imaginable. The book collecting market is quite different from the toy market. In most cases, you likely won't have to pay much more than the face value of the book. One of the books that is worth more than what it sold for when it came out is the hardcover edition of the first novel by George Lucas. In good condition, it sells these days for $20 to $50.

There are so many different Star Wars books and comics, one could spend years trying to piece together a comprehensive collection, especially if you include major magazines that featured the films, such as the "Time" cover with George Lucas.

Trading cards offer another attractive collecting niche. In conjunction with the original Star Wars film, there was a 330-card set released in 1977 by the Topps company that featured subsets broken down by the color of the border: blue, red, yellow, green and orange. This is the most popular and most well known group of cards, and an entire set is now worth $150 to $350.

Subsequently, there were additional sets released for each of the next two films. The Empire Strikes Back and Return of the Jedi sets are not as hard to find and usually will sell for $20 to $30.

In recent years, more trading cards have been released, including the Star Wars Galaxy 1, Star Wars Galaxy 2 and Star Wars Galaxy 3 sets from Topps. These are fairly valuable, with a complete set in excellent condition running up to $1,000.

Millennium Falcon Plate

From a visual standpoint, the newer cards are much more attractive than the older ones. Modern technology allows the companies to achieve special effects now that weren't possible when "Star Wars" first came out.

Another popular aspect of collecting is movie posters. The most valuable posters are the actual promotional ones displayed in theaters to advertise the films. Some of the more interesting and unique (and therefore more sought after and valuable) posters are the ones featuring "Revenge of the Jedi," the original title of the third installment in the trilogy. These are tough find and will go for $400 if they're in good shape.

The original Star Wars poster is certainly a hot item (and will sell for up to $1,000), as is the Happy Birthday poster made for theaters that were still showing the film a year after its original release date. Because of the abundance that have been produced over the years, posters offer a good start into Star Wars collecting. Prices are generally down, and they're generally easy to come by. Any store that sells movie posters will most certainly have a Star Wars item or two.

In addition to the promotional posters, many magazines included pull-out posters. Most of these aren't true collectibles because so many were pro-

duced, but they're easy to come by and certainly look nice on your wall. Many of the magazine posters look as sharp as the theatrical posters, but because of the supply, they don't carry the same value. The "Star Wars Official Poster Monthly" originals are reasonably priced and somewhat easy to find and offer a good source of posters.

If printed materials aren't what you're looking for, there are countless other non-toy-

related Star Wars collectibles out there that aren't that hard to find and won't cost you an arm and a leg.

In the late '70s and early '80s, if you could think of something that could have the Star Wars logo on it, you could find it somewhere. Swing sets, furniture, cups, banks, ceramics, toys, clothing and literally thousands of knickknacks were available to a Star Wars-hungry public. You could literally decorate your entire house, from bed sheets to cups and plates, with Star Wars memorabilia.

Typically, the random Star Wars-related items don't have much value, with a few exceptions. Adam Joseph Industries produced a Gamorrean Guard vinyl bank that is extremely rare and will sell for several hundred dollars.

There are multiple ceramic items from the Sigma company that are fairly collectible, including salt and pepper shakers and figurines. The Yoda salt and pepper shakers and the R2-D2 and R5-D4 salt and pepper

R2-D2 / C-3PO Alarm Clock

shakers are very rare, and anything that features Boba Fett is usually highly sought after.

Other collectible items include Halloween costumes, board games, puzzles, cups, mugs, models and watches.

One rather unique niche of Star Wars collecting is bootleg items. Some of the items from China and the Eastern European countries are fairly nice looking and highly sought after by those collectors who have to have one of everything. One of the most popular items is the line of figures from Turkey, which were not licensed by Lucasfilm Ltd. There are some minor changes that differentiate those figures from the licensed Kenner products. For instance, The Hoth Stormtrooper is blue and is called Blue Stars. In the package, it will sell for up to $1,000.

Another interesting niche of collecting is fast food memorabilia. There's a lot of crossover here — fast food collecting is extremely popular in its own right, and most fast food collectors will be looking for the Star Wars stuff.

Pizza Hutt Darth Vader box

Burger King produced three different sets (for each film) of four glasses each. The Star Wars set is worth the most, with each glass going for up to $10. Glasses from the other sets are usually worth half that amount. Again, if you're looking for the most popular item, look no farther than Boba Fett: The Empire Strikes Back glass with Darth Vader and Boba Fett is the most popular of all the fast food glasses.

Some fast food items were recalled shortly after their release because of safety concerns. Among them, the Explod-

ing Darth Vader in a Taco Bell premium that coincided with the re-release of the films. Relatively few items were produced and now the piece is highly collectible.

The following checklist features some of the more interesting Star Wars non-toy items. Certainly, there are thousands upon thousands of items somehow related to Star Wars not listed here, but we thought we'd include items that are somewhat easy to find, or items that are so highly sought after that they couldn't be left out.

EVERYTHING ELSE (1977-PRESENT)

PRINTED MATERIALS

BOOKS

- ❑ The Art of Return of the Jedi
- ❑ The Art of Star Wars
- ❑ The Art of The Empire Strikes Back
- ❑ Artoo Detoo Activity Book
- ❑ C-3PO's Book About Robots
- ❑ Chewbacca Activity Book
- ❑ The Courtship of Princess Leia novel
- ❑ Darth Vader Activity Book
- ❑ Darth Vader coloring book
- ❑ The Empire Strikes Back Coloring Book
- ❑ The Empire Strikes Back Mix and Match Storybook
- ❑ The Empire Strikes Back soundtrack book
- ❑ The Empire Strikes Back Storybook
- ❑ The Essential Guide to Characters

- ❑ The Essential Guide to Droids
- ❑ The Essential Guide to Planets and Moons
- ❑ The Essential Guide to Vehicles and Vessels
- ❑ The Essential Guide to Weapons and Technology
- ❑ The Ewoks Join the Fight
- ❑ A Guide to the Star Wars Universe
- ❑ Han Solo: The Lost Legacy novel
- ❑ Han Solo's Revenge novel
- ❑ Han Solo: Star's End novel
- ❑ Lando Calrissian coloring book
- ❑ Lando Calrissian: The

- Flamewind of Oseon
- ❑ Lando Calrissian: The Mindharp of Sharu
- ❑ Lando Calrissian: The Starcave of ThonBoka
- ❑ Lando, Leia, Han, Chewbacca coloring book
- ❑ Leia, Chewbacca, C-3PO coloring book
- ❑ Luke Skywalker Activity Book
- ❑ Luke Skywalker coloring book
- ❑ Max Rebo Band coloring book
- ❑ Monster Activity Book
- ❑ The Mystery of the Rebellious Robot

**Chewbacca's Activity Book
Hardcover children's book**

Han Solo and the Lost Legacy
Softcover novel

- ❏ R2-D2 coloring book
- ❏ Return of the Jedi: Collector's Edition
- ❏ Return of the Jedi soundtrack book
- ❏ Return of the Jedi Storybook
- ❏ Shadows of the Empire novel
- ❏ Splinter of the Mind's Eye
- ❏ Star Wars Book About Flight
- ❏ The Star Wars Album
- ❏ The Star Wars Compendium
- ❏ Star Wars: Dark Force Rising novel
- ❏ Star Wars: The Empire Strikes Back novel
- ❏ Star Wars: From the Adventures of Luke Skywalker novel
- ❏ Star Wars: Heir to the Empire novel
- ❏ Star Wars: The Last Command novel
- ❏ Star Wars Mix and Match Storybook
- ❏ Star Wars original movie program
- ❏ Star Wars Question and Answer Book About Computers
- ❏ Star Wars Question and Answer Book About Space
- ❏ Star Wars: Return of the Jedi novel
- ❏ Star Wars soundtrack book

The Empire Strikes Back Mix or Match Storybook

STAR WARS
The Empire Strikes Back™
MIX or MATCH Storybook

MORE THAN 200,000 COMBINATIONS

Illustrated by Wayne Douglas Barlowe

Copyright © 1980 by Lucasfilm, Ltd. All rights reserved under International and Pan-American Copyright Conventions. Published in the United States by Random House, Inc., New York, and simultaneously in Canada by Random House of Canada Limited, Toronto. ISBN: 0–394–84499–8
Manufactured in the United States of America   1 2 3 4 5 6 7 8 9 0

TM   Trademark owned by Lucasfilm, Ltd.

$2.95   **Random House**   394–84499–8

**The Empire Strikes Back
Coloring Book**

❏ The Star Wars Storybook
❏ The Truce at Bakura novel
❏ Wicket coloring book
❏ The World of Star Wars
❏ Yoda Activity Book
❏ Yoda coloring book

COMIC BOOKS

❏ Dark Empire #1
❏ Dark Empire #2
❏ Dark Empire #3
❏ Dark Empire #4
❏ Dark Empire #5
❏ Dark Empire #6
❏ Marvel Droids #1
❏ Marvel Droids #2
❏ Marvel Droids #3
❏ Marvel Droids #4
❏ Marvel Droids #5
❏ Marvel Droids #6
❏ Marvel Droids #7
❏ Marvel Droids #8
❏ Marvel Ewoks #1
❏ Marvel Ewoks #2
❏ Marvel Ewoks #3
❏ Marvel Ewoks #4
❏ Marvel Ewoks #5
❏ Marvel Ewoks #6
❏ Marvel Ewoks #7
❏ Marvel Ewoks #8

❏ Marvel Ewoks #9
❏ Marvel Ewoks #10
❏ Marvel Ewoks #11
❏ Marvel Ewoks #12
❏ Marvel Ewoks #13
❏ Marvel Ewoks #14
❏ Marvel Star Wars Comics #1
❏ Marvel Star Wars Comics #2
❏ Marvel Star Wars Comics #3
❏ Marvel Star Wars Comics #4

❏ Marvel Star Wars Comics #5
❏ Marvel Star Wars Comics #6
❏ Marvel Star Wars Comics #7
❏ Marvel Star Wars Comics #8
❏ Marvel Star Wars Comics #9
❏ Marvel Star Wars Comics #10
❏ Marvel Star Wars Comics #11
❏ Marvel Star Wars Comics #12
❏ Marvel Star Wars Comics #13
❏ Marvel Star Wars Comics #14

**The Empire Strikes Back
Storybook**

The Ewoks Join the Fight
Hardcover book

❏ Marvel Star Wars Comics #15
❏ Marvel Star Wars Comics #16
❏ Marvel Star Wars Comics #17
❏ Marvel Star Wars Comics #18
❏ Marvel Comics: Return of the Jedi
❏ Marvel Comics: Star Wars Special Edition
❏ Tales of the Jedi #1
❏ Tales of the Jedi #2
❏ Tales of the Jedi #3
❏ Tales of the Jedi #4
❏ Tales of the Jedi #5

OFFICE SUPPLIES

❏ Admiral Ackbar eraser
❏ Bib Fortuna eraser
❏ Darth Vader eraser
❏ Gamorrean Guard eraser
❏ Jabba the Hutt eraser
❏ Max Rebo eraser
❏ Mead Chewbacca, Han Solo binder
❏ Mead Darth Vader binder
❏ Mead Darth Vader, Stormtroopers folder
❏ Mead Droids folder
❏ Mead Leia, Luke, Obi-Wan, Han Solo binder
❏ Mead Luke, Chewbacca, Han Solo folder

❏ Mead Luke Skywalker, Princess Leia folder
❏ Mead Obi-Wan Kenobi folder
❏ Mead R2-D2, C-3PO binder
❏ Mead X-Wing, Tie Fighter folder
❏ Mead Yoda folder
❏ R2-D2 eraser
❏ Wickett the Ewok eraser
❏ Yoda eraser

POSTERS

❏ The Empire Strikes Back Poster Art (Dagobah)
❏ The Empire Strikes Back Special Edition

❏ The Empire Strikes Back theater poster ("The Star Wars saga continues")
❏ Poster of action figures
❏ Poster of Millenium Falcon, Tie Fighters and Imperial Star Destroyer
❏ Return of the Jedi Special Edition
❏ Return of the Jedi theater poster ("To a galaxy far, far away")
❏ Revenge of the Jedi theather poster ("The saga continues")
❏ Star Wars birthday poster ("One year old today.")

The Mystery of the Rebellious Robot Hardcover children's book

K48787

$3.50

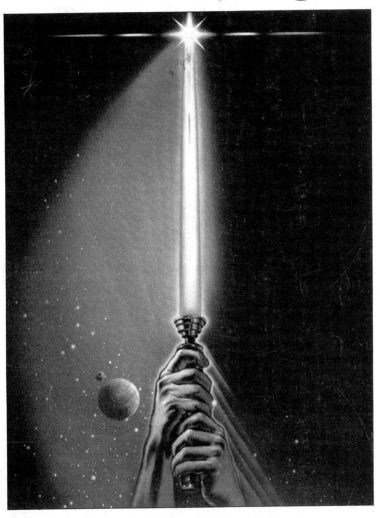

STAR.WARS
RETURN OF THE JEDI

TM: © LUCASFILM 1983 (LFL)   TM

35

0 71896 48787

OFFICIAL
COLLECTORS
EDITION

Return of the Jedi
Official Collectors Edition
Softcover book

❏ Star Wars insider poster
❏ Star Wars Official Poster Monthly #1
❏ Star Wars Official Poster Monthly #2
❏ Star Wars Official Poster Monthly #3
❏ Star Wars Official Poster Monthly #4
❏ Star Wars Official Poster Monthly #5
❏ Star Wars Official Poster Monthly #6
❏ Star Wars Official Poster Monthly #7
❏ Star Wars Official Poster Monthly #8
❏ Star Wars Official Poster Monthly #9
❏ Star Wars Official Poster Monthly #10
❏ Star Wars Official Poster Monthly #11
❏ Star Wars Official Poster Monthly #12
❏ Star Wars Official Poster Monthly #13
❏ Star Wars Official Poster Monthly #14
❏ Star Wars Official Poster

❏ Monthly #15
❏ Star Wars Official Poster Monthly #16
❏ Star Wars Official Poster Monthly #17
❏ Star Wars Official Poster Monthly #18
❏ Star Wars Poster Art (Darth Vader lives)
❏ Star Wars Poster Art (The forces of good and evil)
❏ Star Wars Poster Art (Heroes and villians)
❏ Star Wars Special Edition
❏ Star Wars theater poster ("A long time ago in a galaxy far, far away …")

TOPPS TRADING CARDS

❏ The Empire Strikes Back photo cards (blue border)
❏ The Empire Strikes Back photo cards (red border)
❏ The Empire Strikes Back photo cards (yellow border)
❏ The Empire Strikes Back large cards
❏ Return of the Jedi photo cards (red border)
❏ Return of the Jedi photo cards (blue border)
❏ Shadows of the Empire cards
❏ Star Wars Galaxy 1 cards
❏ Star Wars Galaxy 2 cards
❏ Star Wars Galaxy 3 cards
❏ Star Wars photo cards (blue border)
❏ Star Wars photo cards (green border)

Star Wars Official Soundtrack Softcover book included with album

STARWARS

RETURN OF THE JEDI

**THE
STORYBOOK
BASED ON
THE MOVIE**

Return of the Jedi Storybook

❏ Star Wars photo cards (orange border)

❏ Star Wars photo cards (red border)

❏ Star Wars photo cards (yellow border)

❏ Star Wars sugar free gum cards

❏ Star Wars vehicle cards

ALL THE REST

FAST FOOD ITEMS

❏ Burger King The Empire Strikes Back Darth Vader glass

❏ Burger King The Empire Strikes Back Lando Calrissian glass

❏ Burger King The Empire Strikes Back Luke Skywalker glass

❏ Burger King The Empire Strikes Back R2-D2 and C-3PO glass

❏ Burger King Return of the Jedi Emperor's Throne Room glass

❏ Burger King Return of the Jedi Ewok Village glass

❏ Burger King Return of the Jedi Jabba the Hutt glass

❏ Burger King Return of the Jedi Tatooine Desert glass

❏ Burger King Star Wars Chewbacca glass

❏ Burger King Star Wars Darth Vader glass

❏ Burger King Star Wars Luke Skywalker glass

❏ Burger King Star Wars R2-D2 and C-3PO glass

❏ Taco Bell Millenium Falcon Gyro

❏ Taco Bell Puzzle Cube

❏ Taco Bell R2-D2 Play Set

❏ Taco Bell Magic Cube (Vader / Yoda)

❏ Taco Bell Floating Cloud City

Star Wars: From the Adventures of Luke Skywalker Softcover novel

Can rockets fly to the stars?

Are there moon creatures?

Can humans explore Mars?

**The Star Wars Quesion and
Answer Book about Space
Hardcover book**

❑ Taco Bell Balancing Boba Fett

❑ Taco Bell Exploding Death Star

❑ Taco Bell Yoda

❑ Pizza Hutt Darth Vader box

❑ Pizza Hutt Stormtrooper box

❑ Pizza Hutt R2-D2 box

❑ Pizza Hutt C-3PO box

MISCELLANEOUS

❑ Admiral Ackbar bookmark

❑ Battle at the Sarlaac Pit game

❑ Black Stormtrooper (bootleg)

❑ Boba Fett bookmark

❑ C-3PO and R2-D2 alarm clock

❑ C-3PO and R2-D2 cookie jar

❑ C-3PO bookmark

❑ Chewbacca bookmark

❑ Chewbacca Halloween costume

❑ Chewbacca shampoo

❑ Darth Vader bookmark

❑ Darth Vader, ceramic head

❑ Darth Vader cookie jar

❑ Darth Vader shampoo

❑ Emperor's Royal Guard
   bookmark

❑ The Empire Strikes Back
   French post card

❑ The Empire Strikes Back
   toy catalog

❑ The Empire Strikes Back medal
   showing Darth Vader

❑ The Empire Strikes Back watch

❑ Galaxy Empire (bootleg
   Chewbacca)

❑ Galaxy Empire (bootleg Chewbacca in bounty hunter disguise)

❑ Galaxy Empire (bootleg
   Darth Vader)

❑ Galaxy Empire (bootleg
   Stormtrooper)

❑ Han Solo bookmark

❑ Imperial Stormtrooper
   bookmark

❑ Jabba the Hutt bookmark

❑ Lando Calrissian bookmark

❑ Luke Skywalker bookmark

❑ Luke Skywalker Halloween
   costume

❑ Millenium Falcon plate

❑ Obi-Wan Kenobi bookmark

❑ Princess Leia bookmark

❑ Princess Leia Halloween costume

❑ Purple Princess Leia (bootleg)

❑ R2-D2, C-3PO alarm clock

❑ R2-D2 bookmark

**Star Wars Album Softcover
book**

K 49472 ISSUE 2 $2.95

U.K. £1.25

THE WORLD OF STAR WARS

A COMPENDIUM OF FACT AND FANTASY FROM *STAR WARS* AND *THE EMPIRE STRIKES BACK*

0-931550-71-8

The World of Star Wars
Softcover book

❏ R2-D2 remote controlled, vintage

❏ Red Stormtrooper (bootleg)

❏ Return of the Jedi toy catalog

❏ Return of the Jedi stickers

❏ Ricanelas crackers

❏ Star Wars bed spread (1-3)

❏ Star Wars debut in China
   post card

❏ Star Wars French post card

❏ Star Wars post cards
   (with photos from film)

❏ Star Wars watch

❏ Tie Fighters plate

❏ Wickett bookmark

❏ X-Wing plate

❏ Yoda bookmark

❏ Yoda bubble bath

❏ Yoda, ceramic

❏ Yoda, cookie jar

❏ Yoda costume

❏ Yoda Jedi Master Question
answerer

RECORDS / DISKS

❏ Cantina Band music 45 rpm
   record

❏ The Empire Strikes Back
   (book/record)

❏ The Empire Strikes Back
   medley 45 rpm record

❏ The Empire Strikes Back

soundtrack

❏ The Ewoks (book/record)

❏ The Planet of the Hoojibs
   (book/record)

❏ Return of the Jedi (book/record)

❏ Star Wars (book/record)

❏ Star Wars laser disc

❏ Star Wars soundtrack (album

cover)

❏ Star Wars soundtrack
   (spread from book in album)

❏ Star Wars Title Theme — Funk
   (record from RCA)

❏ The Story of Star Wars
   (album cover)

❏ The Story of Star Wars (album)

TV 446

**The Star Wars Storybook
Hardcover book**

Return of the Jedi
Marvel Comic #1

Return of the Jedi
Marvel Comic

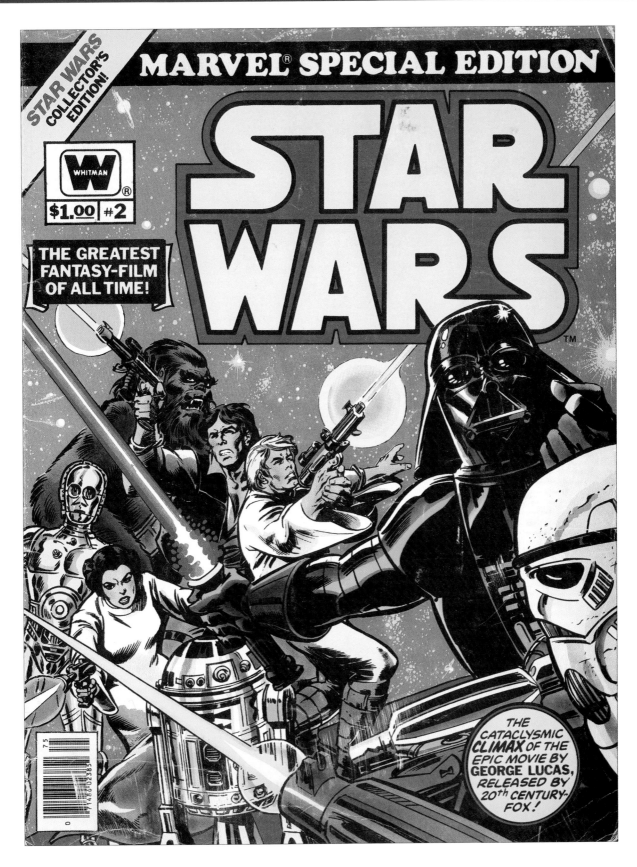

Star Wars
Marvel Comics #2

Star Wars
Marvel Comic
Inside pages

TM:© Lucasfilm 1980 (LFL)

The Empire Strikes Back
Droids folder

Star Wars
Obi-Wan Kenobi folder

TM:© Lucasfilm 1980 (LFL)

The Empire Strikes Back
Yoda folder

The Empire Strikes Back
Official Poster Monthly
Issue One

**Star Wars
Action figures poster**

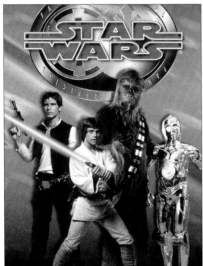

Star Wars post cards

Original art by Howard Cook/Airworks

**Star Wars
Poster**

® &© 1995 Lucasfilm Ltd. All Rights Reserved. Produced exclusively for the Official Star Wars Fan Club. 1-800-TRUE-FAN

**Star Wars
Movie program**

The Empire Strikes Back,
Return of the Jedi
Burger King glasses

Ricanelas crackers

Pizza Hutt C-3PO box

**The Empire Strikes Back
Bed spread**

**Return of the Jedi
Bed spread**

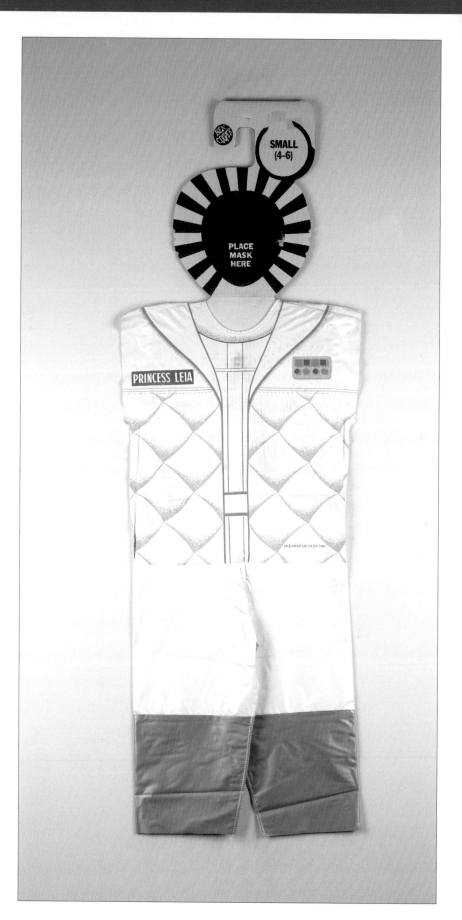

The Empire Strikes Back, Return of the Jedi caps

**Princess Leia, Yoda
Halloween costume**

R2-D2 / C-3PO
Cookie jar

Darth Vader
Cookie jar

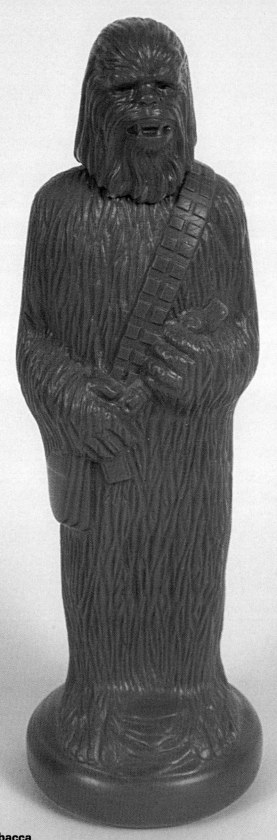

**Chewbacca
Shampoo**

Yoda
Bubble bath

**Darth Vader
Ceramic head**

Yoda Jedi Master
Question answerer

Tie Fighters plate

X-Wing plate

Brian Semling has been active in the Star Wars memorabilia market since 1994. Beginning in 1996, he decided to dive into the hobby full time by opening Brian's Toys in his hometown of Fountain City, Wisc., partly as a source of income, and partly to continue his efforts to reclaim the collection he owned as a child.

"I sold all of my toys at a garage sale and had nothing left from when I was a kid," Semling says.

Like many Star Wars enthusiasts, Brian starting searching for Star Wars items again in the early '90s, slowly piecing together an impressive collection, mostly through science fiction memorabilia shows or mail-order businesses such as his own.

"I was amazed to find that there was actually a market in which people were buying and selling Star Wars items," he says.

Eventually, Semling had some duplicates, which he traded to other collectors for items he was missing. Slowly but surely, the business grew, and now it's a full-time job

Born in LaCrosse, Wisc., and raised in nearby Fountain City (pop. around 900), Brian still lives there and runs his business from his home while attending school at Wynona State University.

When he's not busy selling Star Wars items or pursuing his degree in history, Semling enjoys lifting weights and watching the Packers pursue another Super Bowl title.

Contact Brian's Toys at W730 State Highway 35, Fountain City, WI 54629; (608) 687-7572-phone; (608) 687-7573-fax; bsemling@rconnect.com.

Special thanks to Angie Luker, owner of Star Wars and Stuff mail-order toy shop, and Casey Regent for allowing us to borrow a portion of their collections to photograph for this book. Order Star Wars-related items from Angie at P.O. Box 503, Decatur, TX 76234; (940) 433-8482-phone; (940) 433-5444-fax; SWLUKER@aol.com.